T0360596

Developing Creative Economies in Africa

Bringing together the experience of academics and practitioners, this book discusses creative economies in Africa, focusing on changing dynamics related to working, co-working and clustering.

The contributors in this volume examine how strategies and opportunities such as co-working spaces, clustering and hubs facilitate the emergence of creative industries in a range of African countries, including Kenya, Uganda, South Sudan, Nigeria, Tanzania and South Africa. They also consider the importance of creative intermediaries in providing opportunities and platforms for the development of creative economies in Africa. The chapters present a range of case studies and practices that engage with how creative and cultural producers embrace some of the limits and challenges of their local context to creatively deliver opportunities for economic as well as social and cultural development in their cities and regions.

This book will be of interest to students, scholars and professionals researching the creative economies in Africa across the humanities and social sciences.

All the royalties from the publication of this book will be donated to the not-for-profit organisation the Craft and Design Institute (CDI) (www.thecdi.org.za/) in South Africa, supporting capacity building for young creative practitioners from disadvantaged backgrounds.

Brian J. Hracs is an Associate Professor of Human Geography at the University of Southampton, UK.

Roberta Comunian is Reader in Creative Economy at the Department for Culture, Media and Creative Industries at King's College London, UK.

Lauren England is Baxter Fellow in Creative Economies at Duncan of Jordanstone College of Art & Design at the University of Dundee, UK.

Routledge Contemporary Africa Series

The Fourth Industrial Revolution and the Recolonisation of Africa
The Coloniality of Data
Everisto Benyera

Mobility in Contemporary Zimbabwean Literature in English
Crossing Borders, Transcending Boundaries
Magdalena Pfalzgraf

Advancing Sexual and Reproductive Health and Rights in Africa
Constraints and Opportunities
Edited by Ebenezer Durojaye, Gladys Mirugi-Mukundi and Charles Ngwena

Decolonizing Political Communication in Africa
Reframing Ontologies
Edited by Beschara Karam and Bruce Mutsvairo

Africa in a Multilateral World
Afropolitan Dilemmas
Edited by Albert Kasanda and Marek Hrubec

Developing Creative Economies in Africa
Spaces and Working Practices
Edited by Brian J. Hracs, Roberta Comunian and Lauren England

Implementing the Sustainable Development Goals in Nigeria
Barriers, Prospects and Strategies
Edited by Eghosa O. Ekhator, Servel Miller and Etinosa Igbinosa

For more information about this series, please visit: www.routledge.com/Routledge-Contemporary-Africa/book-series/RCAFR

Developing Creative Economies in Africa

Spaces and Working Practices

Edited by
**Brian J. Hracs, Roberta Comunian
and Lauren England**

LONDON AND NEW YORK

First published 2022
by Routledge
2 Park Square, Milton Park, Abingdon, Oxon OX14 4RN

and by Routledge
605 Third Avenue, New York, NY 10158

Routledge is an imprint of the Taylor & Francis Group, an informa business

British Library Cataloguing-in-Publication Data
A catalogue record for this book is available from the British Library

Library of Congress Cataloging-in-Publication Data
Names: Hracs, Brian J., editor. | Comunian, Roberta, editor. |
England, Lauren, editor.
Title: Developing creative economies in Africa : spaces and working
practices / edited by Brian J. Hracs, Roberta Comunian and Lauren England.
Other titles: Routledge contemporary Africa series.
Description: Abingdon, Oxon ; New York, NY : Routledge, 2022. |
Series: Routledge contemporary Africa |
Includes bibliographical references and index.
Identifiers: LCCN 2021013649 (print) | LCCN 2021013650 (ebook) |
ISBN 9780367481940 (hardback) | ISBN 9781032043722 (paperback) |
ISBN 9781003191681 (ebook)
Subjects: LCSH: Cultural industries–Africa. | Cultural industries–Government
policy–Africa. | Artistic collaboration–Africa. | Africa–Cultural policy.
Classification: LCC HD9999.C9473 A35 2022 (print) |
LCC HD9999.C9473 (ebook) | DDC 338.477096–dc23
LC record available at https://lccn.loc.gov/2021013649
LC ebook record available at https://lccn.loc.gov/2021013650

ISBN: 978-0-367-48194-0 (hbk)
ISBN: 978-1-032-04372-2 (pbk)
ISBN: 978-1-003-19168-1 (ebk)

DOI: 10.4324/9781003191681

Typeset in Times new Roman
by Newgen Publishing UK

We would like to dedicate this book to all the research participants, creative practitioners and academic colleagues we have met during our fieldwork in Kenya, Nigeria and South Africa, as without their support and engagement this book would not have become a reality.

BJH, RC and LE

Contents

Figures and tables

Figures

Tables

Contributors

Damilola Adegoke is a Research Associate and Doctoral Fellow at the African Leadership Centre, King's College London, UK. He is the Head of the Data Laboratory at the centre. He is also the secretary of the TG10 Digital Sociology Board of the International Sociology Association.

Irma Booyens is a lecturer in the Work, Employment and Organisation department at the Strathclyde Business School in Glasgow, Scotland. She formerly held the position of Senior Research Specialist at the Human Sciences Research Council in Cape Town where she led and/ or participated in studies of policy importance.

Andrew Burton is Professor of Fine Art at Newcastle University, UK. He is a practising artist and has worked extensively in Africa, Asia and Europe. His recent projects in Africa include collaborations with artists and 'Jua Kali' artisans in Uganda.

Roberta Comunian is Reader in Creative Economy at the Department for Culture, Media and Creative Industries at King's College London, UK. She is interested in the cultural policy, cultural and creative work and creative higher education. She has published extensively on the role of creative and cultural industries in local development.

Fiona Drummond obtained her bachelors, honours and masters degrees with distinction, majoring in geography and economics from Rhodes University in South Africa. Her masters thesis won the Economics Society of South Africa's Founder's Prize for the best masters by research in the country.

Lauren England is Baxter Fellow in Creative Economies at Duncan of Jordanstone College of Art & Design at the University of Dundee, UK. Her PhD at King's College London in partnership with Crafts

Council UK investigated higher education and business development in UK contemporary craft. Lauren has published research on craft skills evolution, higher education and social enterprises.

Brian J. Hracs is Associate Professor of Human Geography in the School of Geography and Environmental Science at the University of Southampton, UK. He is interested in how digital technologies and global competition are reshaping the marketplace for cultural products and the working lives and spatial dynamics of entrepreneurs and intermediaries in the creative economy.

Emalohi Iruobe is an attorney, entrepreneur, philanthropist and teacher. She is the founder of Tribe XX Lab, the first and only co-working, wellness and incubator space exclusively for female entrepreneurs and female-led organizations in Lagos, Nigeria. Emalohi has a BSc in Finance and Banking from Lincoln University, PA, and a Juris Doctor from Villanova University, PA, USA.

Ndipiwe Mkuzo currently works for the Human Sciences Research Council's (HSRC's) Inclusive Economic Development Unit (IED). He has worked for the Nelson Mandela Institute for Rural Education and Development (NMI), focusing on literacy research in rural Eastern Cape schools, as well as the Fort Hare Institute for Social and Economic Research (FHISER).

Marco Brent Morgan is an urbanist who has worked extensively in policy development and planning, occupying various roles in government in examining the systems of planning in South African cities. He occupies various roles from advisory to operational in organisations such as Open Streets Cape Town, Creative Nestlings and the National Skate Collective.

Lilian Nabulime is a Senior Lecturer and former Head of the Sculpture Department, School of Fine Arts (CEDAT), Makerere University, Uganda. She holds a PhD in Fine Art from Newcastle University (2007). She uses everyday objects to embody a specific social agenda to raise awareness and promote discussion as well as moving the meaning of art beyond the visual.

Robert Newbery is a Professor in Entrepreneurship at Newcastle Business School, Northumbria University, UK. He has worked extensively in Asia, Africa, Europe and North America and has founded and run a number of entrepreneurial businesses having a PhD, MSc, MBA and BSc. He is Head of the Entrepreneurship, Innovation and Strategy Department at Northumbria University.

Wakiuru Njuguna is a partner of HEVA Fund, a creative and cultural economy catalyst fund in East Africa. In her role, she is key to the management of HEVA's portfolio businesses as well as the development of innovative hybrid financial models that combine the best elements of venture capital and impact investment.

Paul Richter is a Lecturer in Innovation and Entrepreneurship at Newcastle University Business School, UK. Paul's entrepreneurship research includes understanding the role of entrepreneurship narratives in framing and developing the careers of creative practitioners; he has carried out projects with these concerns in the UK and in East Africa.

Denderah Rickmers is a PhD student at the Department for Culture, Media and Creative Industries at King's College London, UK. Her research focuses on emerging business models at the intersection of social innovation and the creative industries in Singapore. She is also a Senior Product Associate with the Knowledge & Insights team at the Asian Venture Philanthropy Network (AVPN).

Jen Snowball is Professor of Economics at Rhodes University and Chief Research Strategist at the South African Cultural Observatory. Her research includes work on cultural festivals, cultural mapping studies, employment in the cultural and creative industries and international trade in cultural goods in emerging markets.

Robin Steedman is a Postdoc in the Department of Management, Society and Communication at Copenhagen Business School, Denmark. Her research focuses on work, entrepreneurship and hustling in filmmaking and other creative industries in Africa. Her PhD at the School of Oriental and African Studies (SOAS) University of London examined the work of female filmmakers in Nairobi, Kenya.

Anthony Tibaingana is a Lecturer at College of Business and Management Sciences, Makerere University, Uganda. He holds a PhD in Business Administration, and has an MBA and Bachelors of Commerce. He is an International Development Research Centre (IDRC) scholar and winner of a doctoral award in 2017 from the Production and Operations Society of the USA.

Ayeta Anne Wangusa is the Executive Director of Culture and Development East Africa (CDEA), a creative think tank in Dar es Salaam, Tanzania, and a member of the UNESCO Expert Facility for the 2005 Convention. She is a PhD student in Media and Communication Research at the University of Leicester, UK.

Andrea Wilkinson is a Research Associate at Newcastle University, UK, focusing on Global Challenges and the United Nations Sustainable Development Goals (SDGs). Andrea has a particular interest in how entrepreneurship can support countries to achieve their SDGs and lift people out of poverty.

Acknowledgements

First of all, we are very grateful for the financial support provided by the Arts and Humanities Research Council (AHRC, grant number AH/P005950/1) through the Global Challenges Research Fund (GCRF). The funding allowed the authors to conduct fieldwork in three African countries and establish a supportive research network across these countries and the UK.

We would like to thank our very supportive African colleagues who facilitated our fieldwork activities, contributed to the book or simply welcomed us and shared their views on creative economies in Africa. We acknowledge here their invaluable support in each of the countries we visited.

We are also grateful to all the research participants who completed surveys, met us for interviews and attended our workshops. Their generosity and warmth have made our research journey not only interesting but also fulfilling. As a small token of thanks for all the support and help we have received from colleagues and co-authors in Africa, as editors we have decided to direct all the royalties from the publication of this book towards the work of the Craft and Design Institute (CDI) in South Africa. The CDI is a not-for-profit organisation working across South Africa supporting the development of sustainable craft and design businesses. The book royalties will specifically support their activities in capacity building for young creative practitioners from disadvantaged backgrounds.

Finally, each of the authors would like to thank their families.

Dr Hracs would like to thank Andrea and Henry for encouraging his engagement with the project and being understanding during his time away from home.

Dr Comunian would like to thank especially Leonardo and Jonathan for all the love, patience and support shown during the international fieldwork and writing time. This book is also the result of all their love and care.

Dr England gives special thanks to her parents, Rob and Gill England, for encouraging her to join the project. Also, to her co-editors, Roberta and Brian, for inviting her to join the team.

Abbreviations and acronyms

AFD	Agence Française de Développement
AHRC	Arts and Humanities Research Council (UK)
AUM	assets under management
BERF	Business Environment Reform Facility
BUBU	Buy Uganda, Build Uganda
CCE	creative and cultural economy
CCFU	Cross-Cultural Fund Uganda
CCIs	cultural and creative industries
CCP	creative and cultural policy
CDEA	Culture and Development East Africa
CDI	Craft and Design Institute
DHK	Design Hub Kampala
EC	European Commission
ESG	environmental, social and governance
FCS	Framework for Cultural Statistics
GCRF	Global Challenges Research Fund
GDP	gross domestic product
GIIN	Global Impact Investing Network
GIS	geographic information system
ICCPR	International Covenant on Civil and Political Rights
ICT	information and communications technology
IDFA	International Documentary Filmfestival Amsterdam
KCCA	Kampala City Council Authority
KFC	Kenya Film Commission
LED	local economic development
LQ	location quotient
LSETF	Lagos State Employment Trust Fund
NGO	non-governmental organisation
NOFA	New Opportunities for Artists in East Africa
NPO	not-for-profit organisation

PAC	Pan Africanist Congress of Azania
PPP	public–private partnership
ROI	return on investment
SBD	Sarah Baartman District
SDGs	Sustainable Development Goals
SES	socio-economic status
SIBs	social impact bonds
SIFs	social investment funds
SMEs	small–medium enterprises
SROI	social return on investment
STEM	science, technology, engineering and mathematics
UK	United Kingdom
UNCTAD	United Nations Conference on Trade and Development
UNDP	United Nations Development Program
UNESCO	United Nations Educational, Scientific and Cultural Organisation
UNIDO	United Nations Industrial Development Organization

1 Introduction

Brian J. Hracs, Roberta Comunian and Lauren England

The research journey

This book is the second of two edited collections that have emerged as a result of an Arts and Humanities Research Council (AHRC) funded international research network connected to the Global Challenges Research Fund (GCRF) entitled Understanding and Supporting Creative Economies in Africa: Education, Networks and Policy (2018–2020). The network has allowed the authors to not only engage with the current research, knowledge and practices of African creative economies but also to collect data first-hand about their development and trajectories. We have tried to adopt an inclusive perspective and definition of creative economies, beginning by mapping current knowledge and approaches but also considering how the newly established network could contribute to a better understanding of the sector. We nevertheless remain aware of its limitations, particularly regarding the geographical scope of the book as well as the methodological perspective adopted.

Researching in Africa and writing about Africa

Throughout the project we have been conscious of the claim of researching creative economies *in Africa*. The size of Africa and the impossibility for our chapter selection to represent all its diversity of contexts, histories and conditions is a clear challenge for the research and this edited book. Our research network limited its activities to three African countries, where fieldwork was undertaken in 2019: Nigeria (April 2019), South Africa (June 2019) and Kenya (September 2019). However, within this book the contributions stretch to a broader range of countries, namely Kenya (Chapter 2) Uganda and South Sudan (Chapter 3), Nigeria (Chapters 5 and 6), Uganda and Tanzania (Chapter 7) and South Africa (Chapters 8 and 9). While the

DOI: 10.4324/9781003191681-1

contributions can still only represent a few African countries and case studies, we believe the value of the themes and approaches discussed can not only have an impact across many other African countries but also provide broader lessons beyond the African continent.

Researching complex creative economies

Having previously studied creative economies extensively (but not in the context of Africa), we were very aware that studying creative economies requires a complex understanding of a range of factors and forces across various scales (Comunian, 2019). At the micro-scale, we had previously looked at dynamics of work (Comunian, 2009), learning practices (England, 2020) and markets for creative individuals (Hauge and Hracs, 2010). By extension we were also very aware of the role of place (Brydges and Hracs, 2019) as well as policy frameworks (Comunian et al., 2021) in supporting or hindering the development of creative economies. However, given limitations on time (a two-year project) and resources, the best approach was for us to focus on the meso-level and the role of networks and intermediaries (Hracs, 2015; Comunian et al., 2022) in creative economies. While this remains a partial perspective on the whole system, it nevertheless gave insights into the activities of creative and cultural practitioners (micro-level) and the high-level policy frameworks in which these intermediaries operated (macro-level). This provided a bird's-eye view on creative economies from the perspective of different organisations and individuals that work towards supporting and developing them.

With the specific framework provided by these two considerations, four key themes emerged in our research and exchanges with colleagues and researchers in Africa.

In the first book (Comunian et al., 2021) we considered the role of higher education and policy for the development of creative economies in Africa. In this book we explored the role of creative spaces, such as hubs and clusters, and the working practices, such as coworking and collaboration, that underpin the development of creative economies in Africa.

Defining the sector for inclusivity and sustainability

In order to understand the chapters included in this book and the contribution they make it is vital to define what we mean by *creative economies*. It is crucial to clarify how this term connects with other terms used in the literature and by different authors in this book, namely creative and cultural industries (CCIs), creative economy and creative and cultural policy (CCP).

Since the 1998 DCMS Mapping Document attempted to define the creative industries in the UK, much attention has been paid to trying to measure and define the sector internationally. The creative industries have, however, been considered a very narrow model to adopt internationally and have been widely criticised for their commercial focus (DCMS, 1998). The use of the term creative and cultural industries or CCIs in the book acknowledges a broader and more encompassing understanding.

UNCTAD (2010) and UNDP and UNESCO (2013) position the creative economy in an international framework and as an evolving concept connecting creative activities and goods with the potential for development. We build on the work of UNDP and UNESCO (2013: 12) who acknowledge a "multitude of different local trajectories found in cities and regions in developing countries". We assert that it is crucial to acknowledge that there is not one single creative economy but a multiplicity of creative economies which can feature overlapping and diverging agendas. This accounts for the range of business models and objectives which often expose the connection between creativity and cultural development (Wilson et al., 2020).

In existing literature and policies two often overlapping and fuzzy terms are used: creative hubs and creative clusters. There are multiple definitions of each in the literature (Chapain and Sagot-Duvauroux, 2020) but little agreement on the boundaries and scale of the activities they might include. Adopting an inclusive perspective, focusing not on definitions but on models that make these entities sustainable, might improve our overall understanding. In this book, there is a clear acknowledgement that hubs and clusters need to be understood in context and not seen as top-down policy tools. In many cases, their development and history pre-date the growing popularity of the creative economy and connect to a community-based sociality of work and creativity in those contexts (Chapters 5 and 9). Similarly, their success and impact are shown not to be dependent on specific global business models or formats but on how they are shaped and made fit to address local issues and agendas (Chapters 6 and 9). Therefore, the book does not impose a prescriptive definition, but asserts that the value of these entities is determined by how they are studied, understood and experienced on the ground.

About this book

The book contains eight contributions from a multidisciplinary network involving both academic researchers and practitioners engaged in research across the African continent. They provide a critical platform to examine a range of creative spaces and working practices within the CCIs in a dialogical way, connecting theories to African-specific practices, approaches and challenges. The book is structured in three parts. The first section focuses on creative work, the second considers coworking and the third explores creative spaces.

Creative work: networks, careers and finance

The first part of the book includes three chapters which reflect on the nature of work, careers and business development in different countries (Kenya, South Sudan, Uganda) and industries (fashion, film, visual arts) within Africa's creative economy. Although these chapters highlight some of the specificities of different locations, industries and workers, the findings and policy recommendations are also applicable to wider contexts within Africa and beyond. Combined, these chapters make a valuable contribution to our understanding of the multiple strategies and struggles that allow creatives to make a living.

In the second chapter, Steedman focuses on the challenges that female filmmakers face while operating in Kenya's film industry, including limited distribution networks, access to funding and governmental support. Drawing on eight months of fieldwork in Nairobi, which included participant observation at film-related events and 31 interviews with female filmmakers, the chapter demonstrates how these creative entrepreneurs practise radical flexibility through forms of diversification and crowdfunding. The chapter also highlights important policy recommendations for how the government can help support and sustain the industry.

In marketplaces within East Africa, networks, institutions and supports commonly found in the Global North are lacking and many creatives are sole traders who work in isolation. In the third chapter Burton et al. explore how visual artists construct sustainable livelihoods both *through* art (where artistic practice is the livelihood) and *for* art (where the livelihood enables art practice). Drawing on 21 interviews with a range of working artists from Kenya, South Sudan and Uganda and action research with 60 participants during three workshops in Kenya and Uganda, the chapter highlights the importance of assembling diverse portfolios of work and income streams. Networks, professional mentoring and skills related to curation, communication and entrepreneurship are also crucial and the chapter offers a set of recommendations, including generating more opportunities for knowledge exchange, resource sharing and collaboration, which may enhance the sustainability of the region's visual arts ecology.

In the fourth chapter Njunga et al. examine the role and importance of finance in supporting CCIs in Kenya. In a context characterised by high rates of start-ups by young entrepreneurs, it is clear that traditional commercial financing models that require securitisation cannot work for the sector. Through a case study of HEVA, a Nairobi-based creative finance organisation established in 2014, the chapter outlines the current finance landscape for CCIs in Kenya, highlights key challenges – especially for young women in the sector – and illustrates how new intermediaries can contribute to the innovative development and provision of funding for CCIs across Africa.

Coworking: policy and development

The second part of the book includes three chapters which focus on the emergence, importance and dynamics of coworking within Africa and how it can be used as a tool for cultivating creativity, economic development and social empowerment. Through case studies of spaces and practices within different political and economic contexts, policy recommendations about how to support and harness hubs, incubation spaces and networks are formulated. A key aim is to nuance existing studies on coworking from the Global North by contributing valuable African perspectives and developing poorly understood themes such as the experiences of women.

In the fifth chapter Adegoke and Comunian explore the development and specificities of coworking in the Nigerian context. An analysis of Google Trends data is combined with an online survey of coworking hubs in Lagos and Abuja, highlighting the range of business models and challenges these spaces face, including poor physical and technological infrastructure. In particular, the chapter links four factors – economic, socio-psychological, environmental and technological – to the recent expansion of coworking spaces in Nigeria. In so doing, it provides specific policy recommendations and joins the call made by others for the need to "de-Westernise" knowledge about creative coworking.

In the sixth chapter England et al. assert the need to contextualise the development of coworking and its role in supporting entrepreneurship in Africa with the role of gender. Indeed, while entrepreneurship and coworking are widely spread in Nigeria, women do not benefit from equality at the political level which impacts their access to funding, networks, spaces and mentorship. Data is presented from an in-depth case study, including interviews and observation, of Tribe XX Lab in Lagos, which is the only coworking space in the city that specifically targets women. The case reveals how the organisation seeks to address the challenges facing female entrepreneurs in Nigeria, but also the multifunctionality of the space acting as a platform for activism and advocacy.

In the seventh chapter Wangusa et al. consider the emergence of creative hubs and coworking spaces in East Africa. Insights are drawn from ethnographies, involving participant observation and interviews with managers and creative entrepreneurs, of three specific hubs: the GoDown Arts Centre in Nairobi (Kenya), the Culture and Development East Africa (CDEA) hub in Dar es Salaam (Tanzania) and the Design Hub in Kampala (Uganda). The chapter considers how these hubs contribute to sustainable development initiatives and how they are shaped by the unique ecosystems of the three cities. With respect to policy, the chapter highlights how creative hubs connect with not only local urban policies but also with broader industrial and cultural agendas at the national scale.

Clustering and creative spaces

Broadening the focus on coworking, the two chapters in the third section consider the complex and integrated nature of creative spaces and clusters of CCIs. Here creative spaces are identified and understood with respect to how they contribute to multiple and overlapping agendas such as cultural production, economic development, community cohesion, equality, sustainability, tourism, heritage preservation and education. Beyond mere containers, specific spaces are shown to shape, support and sustain important activities and policies within creative economies and African societies more broadly. Once again, these chapters illustrate the importance of specificity and scale and contribute perspectives from poorly understood rural and remote contexts.

To combat unemployment, poverty and inequality, developing countries have been implementing specific cultural development policies at the regional level that are aimed at growing the CCIs. In the eighth chapter Drummond and Snowball address the developed country and urban bias by focusing on CCIs clustering in a rural, small-town context in the developing country of South Africa. Findings are drawn from a fine-scale audit of CCIs operating within the Sarah Baartman District conducted in 2017 involving document analysis, visual methods such as geographic information system (GIS) and participant observation. The audit identified 1,048 CCIs and a rapid expansion since 2014. The chapter asserts the importance of basing policies on accurate data and determining in advance whether specific small towns are good candidates for culture-led development strategies. For example, it is argued that to increase the likelihood of success, a small town should have an existing CCIs cluster from which to build and should focus on activities in which it holds a comparative advantage.

Further nuancing our understanding of multifunctional creative spaces, in the ninth chapter Booyens et al. provide insights from GugaS'thebe, a multipurpose cultural space which is the anchor of an emerging creative and tourism precinct in Langa, a township on the periphery of Cape Town, South Africa. Drawing on site visits, focus groups with creative workers at the centre and participant observations, it is argued that GugaS'thebe is a transformative space which not only facilitates cultural production, but also stimulates social development. In particular, GugaS'thebe is shown to serve as a makerspace for local creatives, a magnet for tourists and a catalyst for social and developmental spinoffs. Its success and sustainability are linked to the sustained grassroots involvement of locals, and this contributes to a sense of community ownership of the space.

References

Brydges T. and Hracs B.J. (2019) The locational choices and interregional mobilities of creative entrepreneurs within Canada's fashion system. *Regional Studies* 53(4): 517–527.

Chapain C.A. and Sagot-Duvauroux D. (2020) Cultural and creative clusters – a systematic literature review and a renewed research agenda. *Urban Research & Practice* 13(3): 300–329.

Comunian R. (2009) Questioning creative work as driver of economic development: the case of Newcastle-Gateshead. *Creative Industries Journal* 2(1): 57–71.

Comunian R. (2019) Complexity thinking as a coordinating theoretical framework for creative industries research. In: Cunningham S. and Flew T. (Eds) *A Research Agenda for Creative Industries*. Cheltenham: Edward Elgar, 39–57.

Comunian R., England L. and Hracs B.J. (2022) Cultural intermediaries revisited: lessons from Cape Town Nairobi and Lagos. In Hracs B.J., Brydges T, Haisch T., Hauge A., Jansson J. and Sjöholm J. (Eds) *Culture, Creativity and Economy: Collaborative Practices, Value Creation and Spaces of Creativity*. London: Routledge.

Comunian R., Hracs B.J. and England L. (2021) *Higher Education and Policy for Creative Economies in Africa*. London: Routledge.

DCMS (1998) Creative Industries Mapping Document. London: DCMS.

England L. (2020) *Crafting Professionals in UK Higher Education: Craft Work Logics and Skills for Professional Practice*. PhD thesis. London: King's College London.

Hauge A. and Hracs B.J. (2010) See the sound, hear the style: collaborative linkages between indie musicians and fashion designers in local scenes. *Industry and Innovation* 17: 113–129.

Hracs B.J. (2015) Cultural intermediaries in the digital age: the case of independent musicians and managers in Toronto. *Regional Studies* 49(3): 461–475.

Kamara, Y. (2017) Mapping of the status of cultural indicators and statistics in East Africa. UNESCO report, Available at: www.unesco.org/new/fileadmin/MULTIMEDIA/FIELD/Nairobi/unescoculturalstatistics.pdf (accessed 7 May 2021).

UNCTAD (2010) Creative Economy Report 2010. Creative Economy: A Feasible Development Option. Geneva: UNCTAD.

UNDP and UNESCO (2013) Creative Economy Report: Widening Local Development Pathways. Paris: UNDP/UNESCO.

Wilson N., Gross J., Dent T., et al. (2020) *Re-thinking Inclusive and Sustainable Growth for the Creative Economy: A Literature Review*. Available at: https://disce.eu/wp-content/uploads/2020/01/DISCE-Report-D5.2.pdf (accessed 17/04/2020).

Part I

Creative work

Networks, careers and finance

2 Promoting the film industry in Kenya

State support versus entrepreneurial innovation

Robin Steedman

Introduction

Female filmmakers are thriving in Nairobi. They dominate a local industry, based in Nairobi, where they make extraordinary films – from the early classics of Anne Mungai and Wanjiru Kinyanjui through to the Cannes premiere of Wanuri Kahiu's latest film *Rafiki*. The success of women here is all the more remarkable given how marginalised female filmmakers are within film industries globally. Despite the strong feminist stance of much African filmmaking – African male directors from across the continent have been making feminist films since the 1960s (Dovey, 2012; Thackway, 2003) – women have not had nearly as sustained a presence behind the camera as their male counterparts. And while it is "important to recognise how rare it is in the history of cinema that filmmakers from a particular region have *collectively* paid such attention to upholding the value of women and to critiquing patriarchy" (Dovey, 2012: 19, emphasis hers), studying an industry where women have been successful behind the camera is still vital.[1]

Importantly, Nairobi-based female filmmakers face many challenges in their careers, including a lack of profitable distribution networks for their films, limited social support for their career choices, difficulties accessing funding and limited support for filmmaking from the Kenyan government. This chapter will focus on this final challenge and discuss the relationship between this unique industry of female filmmakers and the Kenyan government and the ways in which filmmakers want this relationship to be transformed.

Globally, state support has been crucial for many innovations in filmmaking: "many new waves would simply not have emerged had cinema been left to the devices of the laws of the free market" (Sanogo, 2015: 144). Issues of inadequate funding have long beleaguered African filmmakers, and filmmakers have had to negotiate a gamut of political

DOI: 10.4324/9781003191681-2

tensions when working with financing from "foreign" sources such as France (historically a major supporter of African film) and European film funds (cf. Diawara, 1992; Dovey, 2015; Steedman, 2018). Finding consistent sources of funding across the duration of a career is difficult for even the most established filmmakers. For example, Zimbabwean filmmaker and novelist Tsitsi Dangaremba found she "quickly hit the glass ceiling" once she no longer qualified for funds aimed at promoting "underprivileged African women in the medium" given her success (Dangaremba et al., 2015: 207–208). These facts suggest that the state has a crucial role to play in supporting the development of the film industry in Nairobi.

Yet, there is also the very different story of video film, and particularly Nollywood – an industry that "was arguably in part a response to the absence of the state [...] both in terms of film policy and in terms of its inability to guarantee the personal safety of potential theatregoers" (Sanogo, 2015: 144). High crime rates and the impossible expense of celluloid meant the collapse of conventional filmmaking and the opportunity for a new form of home-based entertainment (Garritano, 2008: 21–22; Haynes, 2007: 1). This industry was built on the infrastructure and networks that existed to pirate foreign films (Larkin, 2004). The first video makers had no formal film training and were instead businessmen previously associated with "commercial video reproduction and exhibition" (Garritano, 2008: 26) – including the pirating and selling of foreign films. The average budget for a film is $US25,000–50,000 (Miller, 2012: 119) and videos tend to be made as cheaply and quickly as possible and can go from idea to market in a matter of weeks (Haynes, 2007: 3). Nollywood films have also succeeded in gaining a vast audience in Nigeria and the Nigerian diaspora, as well as across the rest of Africa and much of the world (Krings and Okome, 2013). The development of Nollywood offers a powerful counterexample to the idea that state intervention is needed for industries to flourish, and suggests that we must also look at the role of entrepreneurship in the development of these industries.

Here it is important to note that the Nairobi-based female filmmakers who are the subject of this chapter do not operate within a video-film model. There is an industry based in Nairobi – called Riverwood – that does, but this industry does not have the financial power or international geographic reach of Nollywood (Overbergh, 2015). Nairobi-based female filmmakers have, with few exceptions (Kinyanjui, 2008), chosen a different model of filmmaking. Nevertheless, when we think of how to best develop and support the film industry in Nairobi we can take inspiration from these two very different models. As I will show in this chapter, it is necessary to think of how entrepreneurship and state support can work together.

Methods and context

Current cultural and creative industries (CCI) research is dominantly Eurocentric and mainstream theorising in the discipline is derived from a narrow empirical foundation based predominantly in Europe and North America (Alacovska and Gill, 2019). Research from other geographies, particularly in the Global South, is thus vital. When seeking to understand African creative industries long-term fieldwork is necessary because "the conceptual understanding of the CCIs across Africa should build on empirical engagement with what exists, rather than with conceptual engagement with industry models and classifications that have emerged elsewhere" (De Beukelaer, 2017: 583).

This chapter is based on eight months of fieldwork in Nairobi (October 2014 to June 2015). While in the field, I adopted two main methods. First, I conducted 31 semi-structured interviews with 27 different female filmmakers (encompassing both directors and producers).[2] Second, I observed film festivals, screenings and professional events to assess how the films of Nairobi-based female filmmakers are exhibited in their local market. Observing industry events also provided vital context for interpreting interviews and seeing how widespread the sentiments expressed in them were.[3]

Nairobi is the commercial and political capital of Kenya, and the city has a rapidly growing middle class (Waldmüller et al., 2016). Technological change, and faith in the power of the digital economy in particular, have sparked widespread optimism in Kenya (Ndemo and Weiss, 2017). But, at the same time, "institutional support for cultural production and digital innovations has not developed" to the necessary level to support entrepreneurs in these sectors (Horowitz and Botero., 2018). In Kenya and across East Africa, government policy "shows a clear lack of prioritization of the creative and cultural sector" and, instead, "a greater emphasis is placed on sectors like agriculture, education and industrialization" (Hivos, 2016). Nairobi-based female filmmakers are thus not working in an environment with strong policy support.

The state of government–filmmaker relations in Nairobi

There are several governmental institutions directly involved in the film industry in Kenya. These include the Department of Film Services (which issues film licences), the Kenya Film Classification Board (that rates films for exhibition), the Kenya Copyright Board (which enforces copyright protections) and the Kenya Film Commission (KFC) (the parastatal responsible for promoting the film industry in Kenya). In this chapter, I am focusing principally on the KFC given its role in promoting the film industry.

Filmmakers widely consider their industry to be neglected by the state and dissatisfaction with the activities of the KFC is widespread. In veteran producer Appie Matere's view, the principal reason filmmakers are "extremely dissatisfied with the Kenyan Film Commission" is that they "ended up taking more of an administration [role], and travelling, and selling Kenya as a destination instead of really trying to build within the industry". This was a position that another long-established filmmaker, Dommie Yambo-Odotte, agreed with:

> Over many years Kenya has been the preferred location for many foreign filmmakers and I know that our government has always tried [...] to create opportunities for them to come here more than they have tried to create opportunities for us to create at home.

Kenya has a history of being used as a film location for major international productions, such as *Out of Africa* and *The Constant Gardener*, and the KFC actively works to court similar-scale productions now because of their financial desirability. The South African film industry, for instance, has a local content sector and a service sector, but "the success of the national industry is based largely on its capacity as a service industry" (Tomaselli, 2013: 242). Dommie Yambo-Odotte captured the issue evocatively when comparing her own film projects to major-budget foreign productions, saying "I become the child of a lesser God in this case" because the financial scale of a foreign project would be so much greater than what she herself could spend.

Big-budget foreign films such as *Out of Africa*, the paradigmatic example, show off the beauty of the Kenyan countryside to audiences and production companies all over the world, and can serve as a major statement about the value of Kenya as a film location and tourist destination (thus garnering future business). Attracting major European or North American productions brings the money they invest while producing in country (hotels, employing local personnel, etc.) but also, and more importantly, it connects Kenya to the *audiences* of these films: namely North Americans and Europeans who might then decide to come as tourists to Kenya. In Kenya, "tourism is one of our biggest foreign exchange [earners] and it's always connected and tied to the film industry" (Yambo-Odotte interview 2015). Attracting foreign productions is valuable for the service companies that would be hired to service those productions. Additionally, it can provide spill-over benefits that indirectly contribute towards industry growth. For instance, producers like Appie Matere and Alison Ngibuini worked in the production departments of major international films and thus gained valuable work experience. However, work on these productions is to the benefit of technical crews much more than creative staff, particularly in high-level roles like directing and cinematography.

This strategy is also difficult because it relies on Kenya being more attractive than other locations. The competition between locations is best captured in the example of "runaway productions" – productions "that are financed entirely by the producing country and only use locations and services in the host country, without co-production participation or significant creative input from them" (Iordanova, 2003: 26). Countries compete with each other to lure these runaway productions, and their success in doing so relies on competitive advantage, and this comes principally through being the cheapest. Filmmakers seriously questioned whether Kenya had created the enabling conditions to compete with other African destinations (such as South Africa and Tanzania) on this front. As Wanuri Kahiu said:

> Even if they were doing Kenya as a destination and nothing else, then they should be lobbying for the government to have tax breaks for other countries to bring in films here. That's what you do if you're doing Kenya as a destination. But you're not even doing that. So you can't even say I'm promoting Kenya as a destination because you're not. Tanzania is giving better breaks.

This strategy of "selling Kenya as a perfect filming destination" is currently "a problem because of Al Shabab" (Wanja interview 2015). The Somalia-based terrorist group has been responsible for a significant number of large-scale attacks on Kenyan soil in the last decade, and this has resulted in large parts of the country, including popular tourist destinations on the coast, being put on foreign travel advisories.

Anne Mungai – the first woman to direct a feature-length film in Kenya – thought it was important progress that an institution like the KFC had been set up, but also that its presence "must be felt". She posed the rhetorical question: "we have it in place, but what is it doing"? In comparison, other institutions such as the Friedrich Ebert Foundation and Goethe-Institut had a tangible impact on the local industry because they supported the development of her first film, *Saikati*. As she says, "we did a workshop, we did a film, we did *Saikati*. It's a film you can see". By implication, the usefulness of an institution designed to promote the film industry in Kenya needs to be measured by the number of films it creates.

The Kenyan government has no system for granting funding to filmmakers. They do offer a loan through the Youth Enterprise and Development Fund called Take 254. Through the fund, filmmakers under the age of 35 (or in companies with 70% of their employees under age 35) could borrow up to 25 million Kenyan shillings (approximately $US230,000). The loan was offered at an 8% interest rate, needed to be repaid within six years, and the film needed to be completed within four to six months. The loan was widely considered by filmmakers to be laughably impractical, for reasons I will now outline.

While the government has taken that step of creating a film-specific loan, they have not taken the corresponding necessary step of "creating an environment for the filmmaker to make money off this film for him to pay you back" (Munyua interview 2015). Without a profitable distribution model in place, financing through loans is unfeasible. As filmmaker Toni Kamau emphatically put it:

> who's going to take a loan for 50 million shillings to do a film? We don't have enough cinemas in Africa, not even in Kenya, to be able to make economic sense for you to launch a film. So how would someone make money?

A loan is workable in other contexts but not for this type of filmmaking, as filmmaker Ng'endo Mukii describes:

> That's the sort of thing that would help if you are starting up a kiosk. I get 100,000 or even 250 whatever, I set up my kiosk, I buy my goods, I sell them at a profit. What I need is that start up money. And after that it should continue to cycle as well, as long as I'm set up somewhere well, I'm getting good supplies, like all this sort of stuff. And that's the way you pay it back. Film doesn't work like that. [...] It's just a totally different market. So I think they didn't change their mentality to think about that.

The filmmaking business operates in a fundamentally different way to the types of businesses that could be enabled by this type of loan.

While being deeply critical of the actions of the government, and more specifically the KFC, many filmmakers also saw a role for themselves in educating the government about what they need for their industry and how the KFC could support them better. As Dommie Yambo-Odotte put it, "for the longest time we have said: 'Oh, the government isn't helping us', we've cried a lot. But I think we didn't really articulate how we wanted them to help". Producer Emily Wanja concurred that while people "hate, and hate, and hate about the Kenya Film Commission", filmmakers have a role to play in educating them. She described the filmmaking landscape in Nairobi as being composed of several niches such as Riverwood, service companies and local TV and content providers and argued "there's nothing we can lose by coming together to petition the government or to make certain demands of the government. I think everyone is going to benefit". This collaborative spirit was key to the success of many filmmakers in Nairobi, and Emily Wanja saw no reason why this could not also be the key to a new kind of more productive relationship with the government.

Working without state support

Nairobi-based female filmmakers work in a precarious labour market where they must be constantly attuned to the potential of new opportunities to develop their ideas into films. Their process has precedents. The "Father of African Cinema" Ousmane Sembène's practice of "'mégotage'—scrounging for cigarette butts, raising bits of money wherever possible, through personal or family savings or loans, perhaps from local businesses or the government" (Haynes, 2011: 69) – certainly comes to mind. But they are not "scrounging" in the absence of better opportunities and more cultural support. Rather, we can see their space as one of entrepreneurial innovation. Producer Emily Wanja put it the following way:

> I always say, you look at developed industries and countries and you say, wow, that's amazing that they've got this going and it's possible to make things work like this. But then you come back and say okay, so how do you make what you've got work? [...] definitely it's not a copy paste kind of scenario. It's kind of finding your own solutions. [...] It's very easy to live in Africa to live in this country and be bitter about almost everything. And almost forget the good things there are. [...] If you ask me, it's a great place for entrepreneurs 'cause there's needs. Every now and then

the system fails, it's an opportunity for an entrepreneur somewhere. In this view, the lack of support for the industry actually presents entrepreneurs with opportunities.

Nairobi-based female filmmakers have responded to their environment by becoming radically flexible in their work and exploring every possible option, including diversifying into different screen media formats, mediums and genres. Other strategies have included making use of the Internet to crowd fund, and applying to transnational film festival funds, such as the International Documentary Film Festival Amsterdam (IDFA) Bertha Fund, or transnational film-funding projects, such as Focus Features Africa First. They must always run diversified businesses to generate a constant stream of work and potential income to invest in new films and build local and transnational networks to seize opportunities. Many Nairobi-based female filmmakers create opportunities for themselves to diversify through running their own small production companies. For instance, at her production company On Screen Productions, Toni Kamau and her partners work on both corporate commissioned projects for major organisations such as the M-Pesa foundation, as well as creative projects such as the human rights documentary *I Am Samuel*.

To give another example, throughout her career, pioneering filmmaker Judy Kibinge has worked across formats, genres and modes of funding. She has made short films for the South African pay-tv company M-Net, feature-length romantic comedies and dramas, several corporate documentaries for clients such as Transparency International and the Nation Media Group, a feature-length documentary about human rights abuses in Kenya and a feature-length drama with One Fine Day Films that premiered at the Toronto International Film Festival, among many other projects. Additionally, she is now the Executive Director of Docubox, the East African Documentary Film Fund, which funds and supports the production of feature-length creative documentaries by East African filmmakers (for a full overview of Kibinge's career, see Steedman, 2019). Vitally, through Docubox's activities Kibinge has taken a guiding role in the development of the industry. She has had more than 15 years of experience working in the industry and draws directly upon it in devising Docubox's activities so that the fund is as responsive to local conditions as possible. Through Docubox the local film industry has been importantly shaped by a female voice – something that is often overwhelmingly lacking in the usually male-dominated film industry.

Looking to the future

Stuart Cunningham et al. (2008: 72) suggest that:

> culture that is beholden to government for support is often unable to sustain itself commercially. This is one of the standard rationales for subsidy. Alternatively, straight subsidy has come under increasing attack as it often leads to dependency and stymies entrepreneurial spirit in the creative industries.

Through their entrepreneurial innovations, Nairobi-based female filmmakers have created a vibrant screen media industry without state support, and thus challenge conventional wisdom about how to support independent filmmaking. Lobato (2010: 338) outlines a trend in the literature where the suggestion is for "developing nations and regions to effectively leverage their cultural assets and integrate them into global economic networks, thus providing new sources of revenue, employment and growth" (Lobato, 2010: 338). He examines Nollywood's informality as another way forward to creating a profitable and sustainable film industry violating all these norms, and concludes that film industries in the Global North "have much to learn from this example" (Lobato, 2010: 350).

Women have been successful within Nairobi's highly entrepreneurial space, and the challenge is to further develop the industry without undercutting the conditions that have contributed to its success thus far. One reason Nairobi attracts filmmakers is because, in Philippa Ndisi-Herrmann's words, "it is easier to climb up the ladder" than in more developed industries. At the same time, as Ndisi-Herrmann also notes:

> If it's difficult to get grants, or get support from your government in any way, whatever small amount [...] it does become easy to say "actually, you know what? I'm going to put my film thing to the side and take an office job, or do this or do that".

It is necessary to recognise the incredible difficulty of making film in this environment, and that there is a potential role for the government to play in shaping this environment. So what do filmmakers want the government to do? How do they want the KFC to promote the industry?

There are some reasons why formal government support would be good for the industry. For example, veteran producer Appie Matere described the difficulties of shopping for funding at international film markets without already having some funding attached to the film:

I discovered [international film markets like the one at Durban International Film Festival] will support a film that has support. That has some money to it. [...] Now if I ever go to another forum, if I ever go to pitch, if I ever go for a co-production, I'll have raised some money before I go.

Government funding is not the only way to raise money, but it is a crucial starting point that Kenyan filmmakers do not have (but many other filmmakers do) and it has the potential to make them less competitive for other sources of funding.

For filmmakers – like those in Nairobi – who do not have a mass market to buy their films, film festivals provide another way of exhibiting their films, building their professional networks (e.g. with international producers and distributors) and developing their careers. Dovey (2015: 8) outlines four benefits of film festivals for filmmakers: first, "modest economic returns"; second, "prestige and symbolic capital in the development of a filmmaker's career"; third, they can facilitate activism around causes the filmmaker supports; fourth, they can generate "interpersonal connections in diverse parts of the globe". Filmmaker Natasha Likimani wished to see the KFC[4] support the production of films that have the potential to show in film festivals, particularly major film festivals internationally, and thus access these associated benefits. As she says:

I would rather they give the prominent filmmakers every year money to do a film. Just like I know Korea does, Hong Kong does. Where they say we want a certain type of quality movie so that every year we can apply to these prestigious festivals. They don't do that.

In this view, the most useful thing the Kenyan government could do would be to periodically create films that could tour the festival circuit and gather financing at international film markets. Here the point would not be on the number of projects financed, but rather on the depth of the financial support. As Anne Mungai said, what matters is creating "a film you can see".

My recommendation for the KFC would be to listen closely to these filmmakers – that is, support a small number of creative films that are capable of travelling to international film markets and festivals. Two organisations within Kenya offer useful models that the Kenyan state could adopt to promote the local independent film industry: Docubox and One Fine Day Films. Docubox offers funding, mentoring and masterclasses for documentary filmmakers and since it started operation in 2013 has produced a spate of creative documentaries, such as *New Moon, I Am Samuel* and *The Letter,* that push forward the discipline of documentary making. Likewise, One Fine Day Films produces fiction features, such as *Soul Boy* and *Something Necessary,* that have consistently been lauded at prestigious international film festivals (Steedman, 2018). These organisations offer a model of filmmaking that *already* works in Kenya. The CCIs are commonly valued because of their potential for job creation and contribution to gross domestic product (GDP) (Hivos, 2016; Morean, 2009), and adopting the model that Nairobi-based female filmmakers want would not directly offer these benefits. It would, however, promote filmmaking as an art and cultural form, and this benefit is no less important.

Conclusion

In Nairobi, filmmakers cannot rely on support mechanisms from the government such as loans or grants to make their films, and they widely consider their industry to be neglected by the state. While some filmmakers were glad to see that the Kenyan government created a film commission and considered this a step in the right direction, at the time my research was conducted, all were disappointed with the direction the commission was taking, with some giving up on it entirely and considering it "all talk". Yet, despite this lack of support and the many other challenges they face (such as the lack of profitable distribution networks for their films), filmmakers have succeeded in building thriving careers in film in Nairobi. They have taken matters into their own hands and built an industry where women have been uniquely successful. The first step in developing policies or other initiatives to support and grow this unique industry must be in listening to what these filmmakers have to say, as it is their entrepreneurial instincts that have built this success. The government may have a role to play in supporting the industry, but, as Dommie Yambo-Odotte says, it should "let the artists run the industry. Allow them to flourish".

Notes

1 Scholars have noted the interesting fact of the existence of a substantial number of female filmmakers in Nairobi (Bisschoff, 2012: 64, 2015: 73; Dovey, 2012: 22; Wenner, 2015: 190), but prior to my own research these filmmakers had not received significant academic attention.

2 The following interviews are cited in this chapter: Toni Kamau (2015), Jackie Lebo (2015), Natasha Likimani (2015), Appie Matere (2015), Ng'endo

Mukii (2015), Anne Mungai (2015), Isabel Munyua (2015), Philippa Ndisi-Herrmann (2015), Emily Wanja (2015), Dommie Yambo-Odotte (2015). My analysis is based on my entire corpus of interviews.

3 For a more extensive discussion of methods, see Steedman (2018).

4 Here it is worth noting that, when filmmakers discussed potential government intervention, they focused their attention on the KFC rather than other industry bodies. This is likely because the explicit purpose of the KFC is to promote filmmaking in Kenya.

References

Alacovska A. and Gill R. (2019) De-westernizing creative labour studies: the informality of creative work from an ex-centric perspective. *International Journal of Cultural Studies* 22(2): 195–212.

Bisschoff L. (2012) The emergence of women's film-making in francophone sub-Saharan Africa: from pioneering figures to contemporary directors. *Journal of African Cinemas* 4(2): 157–173.

Bisschoff L. (2015) Cinema in East Africa: introduction. *Journal of African Cinemas* 7(2): 71–77.

Cunningham S., Ryan M.D., Keane M., et al. (2008) Financing creative industries in developing countries. In: Barrowclough D. and Kozul-Wright Z. (Eds) *Creative Industries and Developing Countries: Voice, Choice, and Economic Growth*. London: Routledge. pp. 65–110.

Dangaremba T., Mistry J. and Schuhmann A. (2015) Tsitsi Dangarembga: a manifesto. In: Mistry J. and Schuhmann A. (Eds) *Gaze Regimes: Film and Feminisms in Africa*. Johannesburg: Wits University Press, pp. 201–210.

De Beukelaer C. (2017) Toward an 'African' take on the cultural and creative industries? *Media, Culture & Society* 39(4): 582–591.

Diawara M. (1992) *African Cinema: Politics and Culture*. Bloomington: Indiana University Press.

Dovey L. (2012) New looks: the rise of African women filmmakers. *Feminist Africa* 16: 18–36.

Dovey L. (2015) *Curating Africa in the Age of Film Festivals*. New York: Palgrave MacMillan.

Garritano C. (2008) Contesting authenticities: the emergence of local video production in Ghana. *Critical Arts* 22(1): 21–48.

Haynes J. (2007) Video boom: Nigeria and Ghana. *Postcolonial Text* 3(2): 1–10.

Haynes J. (2011) African cinema and Nollywood: contradictions. *Situations: Project of the Radical Imagination* 4(1): 67–90.

Hivos (2016) *The Status of the Creative Economy in East Africa*. Ubunifu Report. Nairobi: Hivos. Available at: www.hivos.org/assets/2018/09/ubunifu_report_1.pdf (accessed 21 September 2020).

Horowitz M.A. and Botero A. (2018) Importing innovation? Culture and politics of education in creative industries, case Kenya. In: Servaes J. (ed.) *Handbook of Communication for Development and Social Change*. Singapore: Springer, pp. 861–870.

Iordanova D. (2003) *Cinema of the Other Europe: The Industry and Artistry of East Central European Film*. London: Wallflower Press.

Kinyanjui W. (2008) Kenyan videos: a director's experience. In: Ogunleye F. (Ed.) *Africa Through the Eyes of the Video Camera*. Newcastle Upon Tyne: Cambridge Scholars Publishing, pp. 69–74.

Krings M. and Okome O. (Eds) (2013) *Global Nollywood: The Transnational Dimensions of an African Video Film Industry*. African expressive cultures. Bloomington: Indiana University Press.

Larkin B. (2004) Degraded images, distorted sounds: Nigerian video and the infrastructure of piracy. *Public Culture* 16(2): 289–314.

Lobato R. (2010) Creative industries and informal economies: lessons from Nollywood. *International Journal of Cultural Studies* 13(4): 337–354.

Miller .J (2012) Global Nollywood: the Nigerian movie industry and alternative global networks in production and distribution. *Global Media and Communication* 8(2): 117–133.

Morean B. (2009) *Creativity at Work: Cultural Production, Creativity and Constraints*. 35, Creative Encounters Working Paper. Copenhagen: Copenhagen Business School.

Ndemo B. and Weiss T. (Eds) (2017) *Digital Kenya: An Entrepreneurial Revolution in the Making*. London: Palgrave MacMillan.

Overbergh A. (2015) Kenya's Riverwood: market structure, power relations, and future outlooks. *Journal of African Cinemas* 7(2): 97–115.

Sanogo A. (2015) Certain tendencies in contemporary auteurist film practice in Africa. *Cinema Journal* 54(2): 140–149.

Steedman R. (2018) Nairobi-based middle class filmmakers and the production and circulation of transnational cinema. *Poetics*.

Steedman R. (2019) Nairobi-based female filmmakers: screen media production between the local and the transnational. In: Harrow K.W and Garritano C. (Eds) *A Companion to African Cinema*. Oxford: Wiley Blackwell, pp. 315–335.

Thackway M. (2003) *Africa Shoots Back: Alternative Perspectives in Sub-Saharan Francophone African Film*. Oxford: James Currey.

Tomaselli K.G. (2013) Film cities and competitive advantage: development factors in South African film. *Journal of African Cinemas* 5(2): 237–252. DOI: 10.1386/jac.5.2.237_1.

Waldmüller J.M., Gez Y.N. and Boanada-Fuchs A. (Eds) (2016) *(Re) Searching the Middle Class in Nairobi*. Switzerland: Kompreno Research Reports.

Wenner D. (2015) Postcolonial film collaborations and festival politics. In: Mistry J. and Schuhmann A. (Eds) *Gaze Regimes: Film and Feminisms in Africa*. Johannesburg: Wits University Press, pp. 188–200.

3 Making a living through and for visual arts in East Africa

*Andrew Burton, Lilian Nabulime,
Robert Newbery, Paul Richter,
Anthony Tibaingana and Andrea Wilkinson*

Introduction

Despite the creative and cultural economy (CCE) being presented as central to the growth of East African countries (Fleming, 2014), there is little in the way of systematic data gathered on the state of the CCE in East Africa.

Many artists are sole traders working in isolation, and, for the most part, lack the supportive networks, collaborations and institutions that are common in the Global North. There have been recommendations to develop professional skills within the visual arts ecology, to encourage collaboration and reach new domestic and international audiences. However, despite a growing body of research into sustaining livelihoods in developing contexts (Hopwood et al., 2005), there is no clear data as to how visual artists make a living in East Africa.

This chapter addresses this limitation and, through research conducted as part of the Networking New Opportunities for Artists in East Africa (NOFA) interdisciplinary research project, explores how visual artists construct sustainable livelihoods both *through* art (where artistic practice is the livelihood) and *for* art (where the livelihood enables art practice). Having set out how East African artists make a living, we then explore the areas identified by the artists where professional development would help their careers, and the areas where greater capacity is necessary to develop a thriving visual arts ecology.

Artists and sustainable livelihoods in the literature

Worldwide, artists are increasingly being identified as self-employed (Bridgstock, 2013) and, whilst the international CCE is growing, it remains a precarious place to build a livelihood (Gill and Pratt, 2008; Serafini and Banks, 2020). Artists may build portfolio careers, with creative and

DOI: 10.4324/9781003191681-3

non-creative secondary employment both inside and outside of the CCE (Ashton, 2015). However, to build a sustainable artistic livelihood within the sector, it has been argued that artists need both artistic and entrepreneurial skills, where an entrepreneurial mind-set may be regarded as an extension of creative skills (Bridgstock, 2013; Cobb et al., 2011).

The United Nations Educational, Scientific and Cultural Organisation (UNESCO) has a broad definition in which an artist is:

> any person who creates or gives creative expression to, or re-creates works of art, who considers his artistic creation to be an essential part of his life, who contributes in this way to the development of art and culture and who is or asks to be recognised as an artist, whether or not he is bound by any relations of employment or association.
>
> (UNESCO, 1980)

Notwithstanding such an inclusive definition, many would argue that artists require a specific skillset to create a sustainable livelihood from their practice. They need artistic skills to produce their products and entrepreneurial skills to derive a commercial income (Thom, 2016). This is especially so in a creative economy characterised by limited opportunities for stable employment or career progression; the dominance of self-employment; a high percentage holding part-time employment; and a frequency of second jobs within or outside the CCE.

Combining the entrepreneurial and the artistic for many CCE actors is not straightforward. It is a challenge to adopt a profit-driven model when artists are not driven by profit itself but need to be able to make a sustainable livelihood.

This need for an artistic and entrepreneurial skillset can be problematic for an artist's sense of identity and their relationship between self and work (Bain, 2005; Coulson, 2012; Haynes and Marshall, 2018; McRobbie, 2015). A precarious income has an impact on an artist's sense of identity and they may experience fractured identities due to the need to take on secondary jobs in different occupations in order to survive. This leads to an uneasy mix between a romanticised idea of an artist having a "plurality of occupational identities" and the challenge of maintaining this in reality (Bain, 2005: 42). Notwithstanding such complexities and conflicts, the opportunities and constraints experienced by artists in pursuit of a sustainable livelihood are greatly influenced by the context in which they exist (Welter, 2011). In the next section, we explore the East African context in these regards.

Artists and sustainable livelihoods in East Africa

According to Fleming (2014: 3), CCEs in Uganda, Rwanda and Kenya are regarded as key to "delivering the next phase of growth, increasing prosperity". Furthermore, it can support "greater diversity of cultural expressions to reach new audiences and markets and thus for people to make a living from their creativity" (ibid: 3). The authors recognised that, while the end of poverty is a priority, there is also a need to fulfil the cultural and creative aspirations of citizens.

Kenya has seen progress in setting up independent arts institutions that support artists, whilst Uganda is in the process of evaluating its arts and cultural processes (UNCTAD, 2010). In Uganda and Rwanda the traumas of the 1970s and 1990s have meant that developments are still relatively young. In the continuing absence of a proposed East Africa Cultural Council, very little systematic data gathering on the state of the CCE has been done (UNCTAD, 2010). Whilst "Uganda currently has the greatest experience and infrastructure in place for cultural statistics" (Kamara, 2017: 67), this data tends to miss swathes of informal cultural activity and fails to identify visual art activity specifically.

Whilst the Cross-Cultural Foundation Uganda (CCFU) has been lobbying government to support mainstream culture in all development initiatives (Fleming, 2014), across the region, government policy shows a clear lack of prioritisation of the CCE, despite the huge potential to create jobs for youth, boost tourism and build a cohesive national heritage (UNCTAD, 2010). Such reports identify the potential to build capacity and confidence, to frame the CCE in terms of "value added", as well as outlining specific opportunities to capitalise on, for example, "real flair across the creative sectors ... an increasingly youthful population ... the continued significance of crafts and traditional practice for sustainability and innovation ... [and] women and minorities as key participants in the creative economy" (Fleming, 2014: 7–12).

Barriers to development include a lack of government priority and creative education underpinned by entrenched attitudes towards the cultural sector, which is perceived as hostile to the state (UNCTAD, 2010). As an example of the lack of government priority, in Uganda's national vision for 2040, the creative industries are not mentioned and cultural policy is listed only insofar as it refers to traditional cultures. Artists are often seen to be voiceless and uncoordinated partly due to poor organisation, where there is no collective voice to lobby policy-makers to adopt artist-friendly policies.

The visual arts benefit from CCE-related provisions within the higher education sector, with Makerere University's Margaret Trowell

School of Industrial and Fine Art, East Africa's longest-standing provider of tertiary-level fine-art education. Well-run artistic communities and hubs are seen as a fundamental requirement for a sustainable CCE (UNCTAD, 2010). Cross-country collaborations within East Africa are seen as key to developments within the visual arts community (Fleming, 2014). Working within, or outside of, this framework of support, most artists make their living as individual sole traders, selling their work through a variety of outlets. The British Council report *Scoping the Visual Arts Scene in East Africa* (Standing, 2014) identifies a spectrum of artists represented in the region. This ranges from those who are established, sometimes working internationally and who will often have received a higher education in the visual arts, to those who have had little or no opportunity for formal education or training and little exposure beyond their immediate area. Many of these artists are self-taught or learn from their peers.

The report goes on to identify a number of priorities for development which would better enable artists to develop their careers (ibid.):

1. Professional skills: particularly in curatorial skills, the assessment and analysis of work, critical thinking and writing
2. Practical mentoring: in visual arts project management, especially in planning, communication and marketing
3. Artistic exchange and collaboration: with the objective of stimulating, identifying and facilitating ideas and connections within and beyond the region, promoting sharing and building confidence within the sector
4. New ways of showcasing work: to create different kinds of exposure for artists and their work and different kinds of experience for audiences.

Whilst these priorities have been identified, there remains no clear data as to how visual artists make a living in East Africa. In the following sections we explore how visual artists construct sustainable livelihoods both *through* art and *for* art, before identifying ways to make these livelihoods less precarious.

Methodology

In 2017 funding was awarded from the Arts and Humanities Research Council's Global Challenges Research Fund (GCRF) for the interdisciplinary research project Networking New Opportunities for Visual Artists in East Africa. The project envisioned a series of collaborative activities involving visual arts professionals living and working in East Africa and in the UK who would work together with specialists in entrepreneurship in the CCE. The aim was both to explore how art professionals – artists, art writers and curators – developed and sustained their careers, and to identify the "gaps" in provision that visual arts professionals saw as most critical in inhibiting them from developing sustainable livelihoods in the CCE. These might be deficits in opportunities or resources that, if addressed, would allow for more support for the development of career pathways. Within the context of the GCRF funding, the overarching goal of the project was to contribute to building sustainable livelihoods for individual artists – an international development priority to empower the marginalised in urban and rural communities – and, in the longer term, building capacity in the wider CCE in East Africa. Here, we recognise a sustainable livelihood as the resilient assets, actions and capabilities of an individual necessary to making a living (Chambers and Conway, 1992).

Initial research included 21 interviews with a range of working artists from Kenya, South Sudan and Uganda (Table 3.1) and action research oriented around the development of a toolkit with 60 participants during three workshops in Kenya and Uganda. The interviews explored personal narratives in becoming professional artists, with a particular interest in how they incorporated entrepreneurship into their practice. Through a mixture of presentations and artist-led group work, the workshops explored current and potential art-based livelihood strategies and sustainable opportunities to build visual arts capacity. Following data collection, the interviews were transcribed and then coded for key themes by one author; these themes were then validated by the co-authors. In the next sections, the findings from the interviews are initially presented, followed by the findings from the workshops.

Findings

The project found that artists could be grouped in terms of those who were making their living through art and those who were making a living to enable their artistic practice. The latter group were working in and outside the CCE, and their livelihoods tended to rely on a portfolio of money-generating activities. This section is organised to reflect these two main groupings.

Making a living through art

During the workshops, participants were asked to discuss and present their perceptions on the current opportunities for making money

Table 3.1 Interview participants

#	Name*	Gender	Country based in
1	Aadan	Male	Kenya
2	Berhane	Male	Kenya
3	Subura	Female	Kenya
4	Cali	Male	Kenya
5	Desta	Female	Kenya
6	Eskender	Male	Uganda
7	Faraji	Male	Kenya
8	Gadisa	Male	Uganda
9	Kirabo	Female	Uganda
10	Chausiku	Female	Kenya
11	Ifa	Male	Uganda
12	Jengo	Male	Uganda
13	Kamau	Male	Uganda
14	Lencho	Male	Uganda
15	Abdo	Male	South Sudan
16	Ssanyu	Female	Uganda
17	Isagoma	Male	Uganda
18	Zahra	Female	South Sudan
19	Mirembe	Female	Uganda
20	Gwangoya	Male	Uganda
21	Zwaite	Male	Uganda

Note:* Artists' names have been anonymised.

through art. These have been categorised into five different strategies for artist livelihoods: selling, making, working, teaching and writing. Table 3.2 illustrates the variety of opportunities available to these artists.

Most artists make a living through the pursuit of a plurality of opportunities, constructing a portfolio career. The experience of a painter, living in Juba, South Sudan, where the economic and security situation is unstable, typifies this (15). As well as gaining an income through the sales of his paintings, Abdo sustains a living through commissions for graphic art and design work. Sales of his paintings are mainly supported through patronage and commissions from international agencies based in Juba, such as when a local embassy recently held a human rights event. As part of this event, a workshop was run which provided materials to create art works which were then offered for sale. Abdo's customers are typically embassy staff and the majority of these are foreigners.

In selling art, the tension between artistic practice and commercial practice was evident, as illustrated by Kirabo, an artist based in Uganda: "I don't like the word business although I do need money. An artist has

Table 3.2 Current opportunities for making money through art

Opportunities to make money through…	Examples
Selling art	1. Agents (selling abroad) 2. Commissioned work (non-governmental organisations / corporate / embassies) 3. Private dealers and galleries 4. Exhibitions (private shops and cafes; home displays) 5. Festivals 6. Patronage
Making art	1. Awards and grants 2. Collaboration and cooperation 3. Paid residences
Working in art	1. Art tours 2. Framing artwork 3. Running a studio or gallery 4. Selling art materials 5. Merchandising (T-shirts / bags) 6. Working as a studio or gallery assistant
Teaching art	1. Academic career 2. Workshops and seminars 3. Youth and community skills
Writing about art	1. Content creation 2. Publishing

to make money so that he can make things sustainable" (9). Artists often sell their work informally, through friends, in private houses and in local venues such as coffee shops. This is reflected in Subura's story. Subura is an artist based in Kenya, who started selling art to his friends, allowing for more independence: "I didn't have to go out there and change my song, I didn't have to do that" (3).

Another artist practising in Kenya, Aadan, had a similar experience, although he simultaneously works internationally:

> I call myself a painter, because I do many shows in Europe, too in people's houses, in small restaurants, through friends, and they take some small works from me.
>
> (1)

This informal approach is extended to international settings, where artists like Aadan ask contacts going overseas to take their artwork and look for opportunities to sell their work.

Artists may gain exposure to arts buyers during their formative years while still at art school. There, they learn by trial and error about how to value their work and when to sell. This was the case for Zwaite (21), who recounted his experience while studying an Arts degree at Makerere University, Uganda. He recalled encountering an Italian art collector who would visit the Art department. The art collector paid 900,000 shillings – about £250 – for one piece, returning later and paying nearly twice the sum for a second. Zwaite was advised by his lecturers to create work at his own pace and not to sell any more of his work until he had completed his degree; only then would he come to realise its true value – both monetary and artistic. The importance of managing the sale of his artwork in a way that does not devalue it was a lesson that still guides his practice. Zwaite is an example of an artist who transitioned from making a living *through* art to doing so *for* art. Some years after graduating, he has carved out several "non-art" commercial opportunities that allow him to make and sell his artwork at a time of his choosing.

As is common among the wider visual arts community, some of the artists earn through bidding for and winning awards and grants, such as those relating to paid residencies and projects where they deliver arts-related workshops. Such support may also be as a result of patronage through being located in favourable networks. In the case of Jengo (12), he enjoyed the support of well-networked academics at Makerere University and through them was introduced to international visitors from other universities in the USA and UK. This has led to offers of financial assistance and equipment, culminating in an invitation to visit the USA to give a series of workshops there.

Another common way for visual artists to capitalise on their artistic practice – teaching – was prevalent among those studied. This activity extended from formal lecturing in educational institutions to offering informal classes in community organisations. In Jengo's case (12), this activity has evolved over time from volunteering into regular paid work and training others. In 2002, he founded a small organisation which aims to support local communities through workshops in art and craft processes. Teaching comes with trade-offs for artistic practitioners. It can generate a steady income which can enable space for valuable experimentation with art, but, at times, it can leave little time for artistic practice, as Ifa's (11) and Mirembe's (19) stories illustrate:

> I'm a lecturer and because I have a small income I can survive on I have the luxury of doing certain things … you stumble on breakthroughs that will never have been possible if you are very methodical and following the system and so on.
>
> (11)

you find yourself you have less time ... So, it was mainly teaching and producing work ... If I find like I don't have a full day, then I go in to clay modelling, but if I can have a full day, then I'm going in to wood carving.

(19)

In summary, the overwhelming majority of visual artists who are able to generate a sustainable livelihood *through* some form of art-related activity – selling, making, working in, teaching and writing about art – do so by assembling a portfolio of work by exploiting their artistic competencies in a variety of ways. Berhane (2), a Kenyan artist, is typical in this regard:

> I will probably make 30% of my earnings from selling a commodity, an art commodity Most of the other income would come from a research grant or somebody would ask me to make work that is off, not necessarily at work, but it's within the artistic field. It might be design work. It may be a layout for a catalogue.

Making a living for art

It is often difficult for artists to make their living only through art and there were a number of examples in this study where visual artists worked in non-artistic occupations in order to survive and support their artistic practice. Here, they took on a range of roles, including in administration, cleaning, farming, gardening and shop keeping. Desta, a curator and visual artist (5), is typical of this group, surviving from other jobs: "So I also do other jobs for people ... I do like an assistant, administrative assistant jobs. So organise other things for people who are not necessarily ... within the art".

More so, perhaps, than the group of visual artists analysed above, the contrast between how they feel towards the work they are compelled to do in order to survive and their artistic practice is stark. This can be seen in the words of Faraji (7):

> I grow trees, I sell trees ... I do fruit salad and I deliver food to offices in Nairobi... In the evening from 12 at noon, from noon to late night I will do what I love.

At other times, art work and non-art work appear complementary to building a sustainable livelihood. The experience of Zwaite (21), a Ugandan sculptor, is illustrative here. On graduating, he sold his degree work and invested the proceeds. He bought a car and removed the seats when he needed to transport junk and artwork, replacing them to ferry tourists from the airport. He started two construction companies to build "custom homes" using his experience of construction sites when he was younger. Zwaite now estimates that he spends around 80% of his time running his businesses – what he calls protecting his profession – and the remaining time on his artwork.

The project encountered examples of artists taking on work that did not rely on their artistic competence although it was located within the CCE and, as such, non-pecuniary benefits to their arts practice emerged. This reflects Jengo's (12) story. After training as an accountant, he moved to Kampala in 1998 to find work. Unable to find employment in this profession, a friend found him a job as a studio assistant in the Art School at Makerere University. Since then, he has continued to support his wife and family of six children from the income he generates doing cleaning work and selling his artwork. On a typical day, he starts his cleaning work early, leaving at lunchtime to work on his art. Whilst his regular job is crucial in providing a regular income, working in the Art School benefits his art business as the proximity to students and academics has enabled him to develop skills and knowledge as an artist which he now utilises to impact others in his community.

Overall, the findings of this project demonstrate that it is possible to make a living solely through art practice, but there are many more examples of mixed-portfolio livelihoods, where artists derive income from their artistic practice and, or exclusively, through non-artistic practice. Given the resource constraints and institutional "structural holes" present in sub-Saharan Africa (Jones et al., 2018; Kimmitt et al., 2019), the data from this project supports the argument that livelihoods dependent on artwork are notably precarious (Gill and Pratt, 2008; Serafini and Banks, 2020).

Findings from the workshops

Data from the interviews helped establish a more fine-grained picture of the strategies visual artists employ in order to maintain an artistic practice than extant literature provides. The workshop-based research opened up a complementary set of discussions concerned with the wider arts ecology. This requires attention and resourcing in order that visual artists in this region of East Africa might encounter more opportunities to develop their practice and be less reliant on non-artistic employment to make a living. The following section highlights the critical areas of the arts ecology highlighted and identified by workshop participants, thereby representing a valuable focus for future development and workshops.

East African arts mentoring

Professional mentoring is important as it provides role models and access to a successful arts practice, and helps build the networks that are important for accessing opportunities and resources. As part of the NOFA workshops, we explored different models of mentoring – African-to-African and UK–African mentoring relationships. Given the precarity of artists in East Africa, local artist mentors were hard to access. We addressed this by inviting mentors from the East African and South African diaspora. The mentees were given mentor biographies and selected their own mentor where possible. Feedback from mentees reflecting on the workshop experience suggests the intervention has had a productive effect on their practice. As this mentee reported:

> I would like to thank the project for firing up my writing. From the time we had the first workshop, I have been more prolific than I was before. Every day, I wake up as a writer, and endeavour to live up to that name: I write.

Another mentee reflected on how the skills they had gained through the workshops "came from the mentors and also from my fellow participants". They could also "foresee a situation whereby I will continue collaborating with my mentor even after the workshop". These comments emphasise the importance of bringing practitioners together to develop sector capacity and generate new prospective collaborations.

Networking and collaboration

There is research that shows that self-employed individuals are often isolated (Lin, 2014), regardless of profession, and this will be exacerbated with artists that spend much of their time committed to individual artistic practice. The participants welcomed the time and space afforded by the workshops as it allowed them to break out of this isolation for short periods. The workshops also enabled them to see how their peers work and seek opportunities. Research on networks shows how they are valuable in helping reduce isolation, discover opportunities, share knowledge (artistic and entrepreneurial) and lead to collaborative work (Newbery et al., 2013, 2015). Mechanisms to support and facilitate an ongoing programme of networking events should be encouraged.

Entrepreneurship skills deficit

Entrepreneurship has been defined as the skillset that is required when individuals interact with an opportunity (Shane and Venkataraman, 2000). The artists were keen to think through opportunities and explore entrepreneurial techniques and tools. Whilst a number of different opportunities were identified during the workshops and recognised by the interviewees, many of these seemed distant and abstract. This was particularly so for *selling art*, where the opportunities for exhibiting and selling artwork were regarded as limited. In terms of entrepreneurial operational skills, the artists enthusiastically embraced a session where the Business Model Canvas (Osterwalder et al., 2010) was introduced. This is a visual and design-led approach to modelling key areas required to develop a viable business. Entrepreneurial and business skills have been highlighted elsewhere as critical for sustainable arts-based livelihoods (Thom, 2016). The project's findings build on existing research (Fleming, 2014; Standing, 2014) to conclude that there is a need to include complementary and appropriate entrepreneurship skill development alongside artistic skill development.

Curating skills deficit

The workshop participants highlighted curating as a skill that needed to be developed for a vibrant visual arts ecology to emerge. The absence of a cadre of experienced and confident East African professional curators constrains many of the processes and activities vital to developing a thriving visual arts ecology: developing skills in cultural project management, researching East African artists, promoting and commercialising exhibitions, engaging with professional stakeholders and new audiences, etc. Equally, it inhibits the development of critical thinking necessary to develop intellectual curatorial themes specifically relevant within the context. Without curatorial advocacy, there can be a reluctance on the part of galleries to stage risk-taking or innovative projects. The words of a leading Uganda-based arts organisation Director emphasise the significance of growing the region's curatorial capacity:

> Developing curating skills [in Uganda] is key to the establishment of a sustainable visual art ecology ... Curators are job creators and market movers: when they develop exhibitions they bring attention to artists, some who might otherwise not have been recognised, or are unable to meet the barriers to entry to the professional art world. They present artists to potential buyers and give them vital

exposure through publications and the media – growing the art market and artists' earning potential.

(Teesa Bahana, Director of 32 Degrees)

The current situation is characterised by a pattern of "one-off" projects, often organised under the auspices of overseas cultural bodies where non-East African voices dominate, with the risk that the creative and intellectual contexts within which work is situated may not be those that resonate most directly with the creators of the work, or their audiences. Many projects leave little legacy (a key role of the curator), and tend to privilege "known" artists, excluding new talent and reinforcing gender imbalances prevalent at senior levels in the art ecology.

Artistic writing deficit

The participants highlighted that a fundamental constraint to addressing various needs in the visual arts ecology is a deficit in "art-writing" skills. This deficit is apparent at all levels in the visual arts ecology and has multiple impacts, ranging from a lack of confidence in preparing basic written material for self-promotion which can exclude or disadvantage many artists when trying to access professional opportunities, to the absence of a shared body of developed artistic critique needed to underpin a cohesive intellectual foundation for the transmission of contemporary artistic practice within society. Alongside art education, this contributes to a shared understanding which is vital to the appreciation and valuation of art within a society. The deficit within East Africa impedes art professionals in the development of their careers and impacts negatively on the broader development of an infrastructure for the visual arts. It is also likely to contribute to a perceived lack of respect for and esteem of the artist.

Conclusion

The following quote from practising artist and educator (and chapter co-author), Lilian Nabulime, summarises the rather bleak situation in this region of Africa:

It remains the case that visual art is not a central part of East African culture. [...] most people have no interest in buying or promoting art. For the most part it is expatriates who buy art and NGOs [non-governmental organisations] who sometimes commission art projects. There is no Government support and few channels for information that might help artists learn how to improve their situation.

(Lilian Nabulime, 2020)

Interviewees and workshop participants noted that things are improving: the art scene is growing and becoming more vibrant; artists are selling more than in the past; and there are a few new galleries that market and sell art abroad. Increasingly, there are opportunities for artists to participate in local and international exhibitions and attend workshops and residencies. There are more organisations supporting artists that offer opportunities for training and professional development – for instance, in terms of writing funding applications – and artists are learning that they can advertise and sell their work via social media. Artists also recognise that there are opportunities for creating art that people understand as relevant to their particular situations, or that can be promoted among communities with certain needs or issues.

A set of recommendations emerge from the project and the review of literature in this area which it is argued will benefit the sustainable development of the visual arts ecology in East Africa. First, there is a need for the further development of contextually relevant mentoring programmes that enable successful East African and diaspora art practitioners to support developing East African artists. Second, there would be benefit in the provision of a variety of opportunities for East African arts practitioners to meet, exchange ideas and knowledge, share resources and build collaborations, both within and across East African countries. Third, resources need to be marshalled to facilitate and develop an entrepreneurial mind-set amongst artists in East Africa, where commercial opportunities and practices are complementary to a sustainable art livelihood. Simultaneously, there is a need to address the curating skills deficit to create a cadre of experienced, critical brokers and connectors in East Africa. Fourth, more effort is required to combat the arts-writing deficit to enable artists to fully embrace domestic and international opportunities and enrich the regional "art conversation" that is vital to art appreciation and valuation in society. Finally, it is argued that there needs to be movement away from the prevalence of non-East African voices in the curatorial and arts-writing communities in order to enhance the critical artistic voice of the region's visual arts sector.

References

Ashton, D. (2015). Creative work careers: pathways and portfolios for the creative economy. *Journal of Education and Work*, 28(4): 88–406.

Bain, A. (2005). Constructing an artistic identity. *Work, Employment and Society*, 19(1): 25–46.

Bridgstock, R. (2013). Professional capabilities for twenty-first century creative careers: lessons from outstandingly successful Australian artists and designers. *International Journal of Art and Design Education*, 32(2): 176–189.

Chambers, R. and Conway, G. (1992). Sustainable Rural Livelihoods: Practical Concepts for the 21st Century. IDS Discussion Paper 296, Brighton: IDS.

Cobb, P., Hogan, F. and Royce, M. (2011). *The Profitable Artist: A Handbook for All Artists in the Performing, Literary, and Visual Arts*. New York: Skyhorse Publishing.

Coulson, S. (2012). Collaborating in a competitive world: musicians' working lives and understandings of entrepreneurship. *Work, Employment and Society*, 26(2): 246–261.

Fleming, T. (2014). Scoping the Creative Economy in East Africa. British Council. Retrieved 22/07/2020 from www.britishcouncil.org/sites/default/files/scoping-creative-economy-east-africa.pdf.

Gill, R. and Pratt, A. (2008). In the social factory? Immaterial labour, precariousness and cultural work. *Theory, Culture and Society*, 25(7–8): 1–30.

Haynes, J. and Marshall, L. (2018). Reluctant entrepreneurs: musicians and entrepreneurship in the 'new' music industry. *The British Journal of Sociology* 69(2): 459–482.

Hopwood, B., Mellor, M. and O'Brien, G. (2005). Sustainable development: mapping different approaches. *Sustainable Development*, 13(1): 38–52.

Jones, P., Maas, G., Dobson, S., Newbery, R., Agyapong, D. and Matlay, H. (2018). Entrepreneurship in Africa, Part 2: entrepreneurial education and ecosystems. Special Issue: *Journal of Small Business and Enterprise Development*, 25(4): 550–553.

Kimmitt, J., Munoz, P. and Newbery, R. (2019). Entrepreneurship, prospective prosperity and poverty amelioration: the enabling role of conversion factors. *Journal of Business Venturing*, 35(4), https://doi.org/10.1016/j.jbusvent.2019.05.003.

Lin, H. (2014). Contextual factors affecting knowledge management diffusion in SMEs. *Industrial Management and Data Systems*, 114(9): 1415–1437.

McRobbie, A. (2015). *Be Creative: Making a Living in the New Culture Industries*. Cambridge, UK: Polity Press

Newbery, R., Gorton, M., Phillipson, J. and Atterton, A. (2015). Sustaining local business associations: understanding the benefit bundles sought by members. *Environment and Planning C*, 34(7): 1267–1283.

Newbery, R., Sauer, J., Gorton, M., Phillipson, J. and Atterton J. (2013). The determinants of performance of business associations in rural settlements in the UK. *Environment and Planning A*, 45(4): 967–985.

Osterwalder, A., Pigneur, Y. and Clark, T. (2010). *Business Model Generation: A Handbook for Visionaries, Game Changers, and Challengers*. Strategyzer series. Hoboken, NJ: John Wiley.

Serafini, P. and Banks, M. (2020). Living precarious lives? Time and temporality in visual arts careers. *Culture Unbound*, 12(2): 351–372.

Shane, S. and Venkataraman, S. (2000). The promise of entrepreneurship as a field of research. *Academy of Management Review*, 25(1): 217–226.

Standing, K. (2014). Scoping the Visual Arts Scene in East Africa. British Council. Retrieved 19/08/20 from www.britishcouncil.org/sites/default/files/visual_arts_scoping.pdf.

Thom, M. (2016). Crucial Skills for the Entrepreneurial Success of Fine Artists. Working Paper, Institut für Mittelstandsforschung (IfM), Bonn.

UNCTAD. (2010). Creative Economy: A Feasible Development Option. United Nations Report. Retrieved 20/08/20 from https://unctad.org/en/Docs/ditctab20103_en.pdf. URL_ID=13138&URL_DO=DO_TOPIC&URL_SECTION=201.html

UNESCO. (1980). Recommendation Concerning the Status of the Artist. Legal Instruments. Retrieved 04/05/2018 from http://portal.unesco.org/en/ev.php.

Welter, F. (2011). Contextualizing entrepreneurship – conceptual challenges and ways forward. *Entrepreneurship Theory and Practice*, 35(1): 165–184.

4 Financing cultural and creative industries in Kenya

Challenges, opportunities and the case of HEVA

Wakiuru Njuguna, Roberta Comunian, Brian J. Hracs and Denderah Rickmers

Introduction

Existing literature widely recognises that the growth and development of cultural and creative industries (CCIs) depend on a complex interdependency of factors, such as skills, space, knowledge and markets. Alongside these, another essential – yet often underestimated – factor is finance, manifesting itself in elements such as the availability and amount of financial resources provided and the structure of the financial instruments deployed (Mokuolu et al., 2021).

The Global North is experiencing changing patterns of financing for the CCIs with new strategies and priorities of the public sector (Monclus, 2015). Meanwhile, in the Global South it is possible to observe the correlation between a long-standing gap of public funding and support for the CCIs – compared to other sectors and structural issues – and a lack of financial instruments for their development (Mokuolu et al., 2021). However, innovative approaches and pathways to CCIs finance do not have to follow a specific pattern or mode of development; new opportunities and best practices can develop in relatively short periods through both international collaborations and the work of local intermediaries (Comunian et al., 2022).

East Africa represents an interesting context to consider CCIs and finance. It has a growing population and expanding youth (Mokuolu et al., 2021); however, Africa's share of the global creative economy stands at less than 1%. These findings point both to underinvestment in the CCIs on the continent, as well as to its potential for growth. With young people being the largest players in the CCIs, and start-ups and early-stage businesses being predominant, it is evident that traditional

DOI: 10.4324/9781003191681-4

commercial financing models that require securitisation cannot work for the sector. Driven by a growing middle class, significant youth population, a high rate of urbanisation and innovation and the African continent's rapid expansion into mobile phone and internet access, Africa's CCIs are set on an exponential growth path.

This chapter reflects on the case study of HEVA – a Nairobi-based creative finance organisation – to illustrate how new intermediaries can contribute to the innovative development and provision of funding for CCIs in Africa. It looks at the funding landscape for CCIs in Kenya and acknowledges the lack of facilities before the HEVA fund was developed.

The chapter is structured into five parts. Firstly, we consider the broader field of finance for CCIs and new forms of finance (loan-based and social finance-based) globally. Secondly, we focus on Africa and consider the reality of CCI finance there, focusing on East Africa and Kenya. In the third part, we explore the case study of HEVA and provide insights into this history and work. In the fourth part, we detail more specifically the financial instruments developed by HEVA. Finally, we consider the opportunities that finance can offer to the development of CCIs in Africa and the challenges across a continent with very different policies and lack of support frameworks for CCIs.

Financing cultural and creative industries: new modes of intervention

Funding and finance for CCIs have received more attention in the last decade – especially in the wake of the impact of the 2008 global financial crisis. Indeed, a 2014 report by the European Commission (EC) identified as many as 169 separate schemes across Europe alone that aimed at facilitating access to finance for the sector (Dümcke et al., 2014). This trend is also recognisable internationally, with many organisations actively researching ways to incentivise and increase private investments in the CCIs (UNESCO, 2015). Although promoting access to finance is a priority in Europe (Monclus, 2015), Ministries of Culture often lack the legal capacity, or technical competencies, to lend to the CCIs. Hence, financial intermediaries are incentivised via public programmes to engage with the sector using specific financial instruments – such as loan guarantees – and thus, through public or semi-public organisations, mediating between these agencies and the CCIs. Direct public funding is being reduced and the role of financial intermediaries is growing in the creative ecosystem.

Within western countries for many subsets of the CCIs, e.g. the visual and performing arts, a failed market assumption prevails, resulting in the ongoing need for financial support. This has traditionally taken the form of public funds, philanthropic grants, finance by patronage or other financial instruments. Though there was a notional shift in the 1980s and 1990s from "funding" the CCIs to "investments" in the market, this was often not linked to an explicit expectation of direct economic returns (Monclus, 2015), which in turn missed the core of the majority of prevailing financial instruments.

The relationship between repayable finance and the CCIs

There are multiple dimensions that hinder the utilisation of repayable finance in the CCIs today. From an investor's perspective, the CCI dynamics do not conform to conventional finance's logic. They are often unpredictable and unforeseeable, making investing in the CCIs a high-risk activity (Vogel, 2010). This closely interlinks with the infinite variety property inherent to CCIs goods, basically requiring that "each cultural product should be regarded as unique" (Caves, 2000, p. 6). This generates value for creative outputs but also hinders the ability to attract equity investors and debt providers. Today the financial sector is reluctant to support the CCIs for four reasons:

1. A high degree of expertise in each creative field is required to assess deals.
2. Only large, developed markets offer enough volumes, profits and businesses to attract loan ticket sizes that the majority of investors work with.
3. Assets are often intangible, which impedes default securitisation.
4. The scalability of businesses, and other factors prevalent for investment decisions, are not necessarily the objectives of creative enterprises and cultural organisations (Caves, 2000; Monclus, 2015).

From a CCI perspective, for a long time, there has been an underlying, mutual distrust and the financial sector was deemed a "politically objectionable partner" (Monclus, 2015, p. 89). From a CCI perspective, the creative sector is reluctant to engage with traditional finance for five reasons:

1. Lack of financial expertise and business acumen of creative entrepreneurs
2. Lack of financial instruments that address operational realities in CCIs, e.g. offer revenue-based or flexible repayments

3. Reactive business models shaped according to e.g. grant-giving bodies and fundraising frameworks, as opposed to a clear mission, irrespective of the source of funding
4. A gap of available and appropriate capital. Often CCI businesses require less than £25,000 funding, yet investors predominantly offer loans of £150,000 and upwards
5. A reluctance to take on the risk of repayable finance as opposed to grants (Creative United, 2018).

Nevertheless, multiple factors lie behind a rising mutual interest in collaboration. First of all, the notion of "industry" links the CCI to the information society discourse and gives it an enhanced economic profile. This, in turn, led institutions to reposition themselves towards competitiveness and economic development, hence likely raising their profile for investors. Further, per definition technology and innovation-heavy sectors and organisations are part of the CCIs. Finally, public spending and patronage for the arts are dwindling and the resulting funding gaps are enormous (European Commission, 2013) and have not yet been satisfactorily addressed by the private sector, resulting in unrealised market potential.

Until recently, CCIs relied on public funding and other forms of non-repayable finance (NESTA, 2018; Nguyen, 2020). They have been subject to great influence from governments and those individuals, groups or institutions that have the financial means to stipulate grants, scholarships or other forms of non-repayable finance. Funding factors may encompass excellence, quality, access and national prestige amongst others (Monclus, 2015) but, especially for the core CCIs, do not necessarily translate into social factors and much less so measurable social impacts. Moreover, as patronage and public funding are decreasing in the Global North (Upstart Co-lab, 2017), they are often not available in the Global South altogether.

In this climate, investment decisions are based on measurable, often financial, parameters and business language rather than artistic potential or cultural value. In response to a budget debate, the National Endowment for the Arts – the US governmental agency for arts and cultural sector funding – for example, created the #morethanart campaign, which selected and promoted projects based on their potential return on investment, with a focus on those with a commercial or economic component (Nguyen, 2020). This highlights the influence of managerial skills, business acumen and capital, as opposed to values traditionally found in the CCIs such as training, skill development and creativity. Thus, business expertise is increasingly important within the creative sector (Hracs, 2015). Business plan competitions that are run by art schools or national organisations demonstrate the importance of being both skilful creators and educated managers, able to actively attract and manage financial capital beyond singular, project-specific grants.

The growth of social finance in the CCIs

Financial resources have been and will continue to be one of the essential resources to facilitate creativity in the CCIs, grounding the romance of the arts in the realities of the economy. With the continued growth and development of the CCIs, creative enterprises are developing novel and sophisticated business models and are, in turn, in need of new forms of capital (European Commission, 2013; Upstart Co-lab, 2017). At the same time, there is a growing recognition that creative enterprises may have multiple and overlapping aims connected to creativity, personal considerations but also broader economic, social, environmental and cultural impacts.

Funding and capital structures can purposely drive and support social endeavours embedded in the CCIs in the long run, enrich methods to measure socio-economic impact and foster knowledge exchange across industries. Therefore, the type of finance employed by a company arguably influences its development and, by extension, can inhibit or foster its ability to engage with and shape social impact and change, from the local community level to the international stage.

The link between finance and social impact is described by Sir Ronald Cohen, one of the initial creators of social impact bonds (SIBs),[1] stating: "if in the 19th century, people spoke in terms of financial return alone, and the 20th century we brought the dimension of risk and return, in the 21st century, we've brought the third dimension of impact" (Kenny, 2015, p. 1:23), highlighting the conscious consideration and measurement of social impact, just like risk and return, in investment decisions and when developing financial instruments and vehicles. Hand in hand with that goes a growing trend towards financial quantification – the growing desire to quantify the financial value of the social and/or environmental impact of an investment, to which the rise of SIBs and other payment-for-success structures are a testament.

Social finance describes the provision and use of private capital to address social challenges and generate social as well as financial returns, addressing the "three Cs – capital, capacity and culture change" – in a single process (ACEVO, 2010, p. 19). This convergence facilitates an exchange of ideas and values and "the integration of private capital with public and philanthropic support to generate new and better approaches to creating social value" (Phills, Deiglmeier and Miller, 2008, p. 43). Social investment approaches range from venture philanthropy and environmental, social and governance (ESG)-investing, to impact investing and well-known social finance vehicles include SIBs or social investment funds (SIFs). Generally, the approach taken depends on the financial return on investment (ROI) and social return on investment (SROI) expectations of the investor, as well as their risk appetite.

According to the Global Impact Investing Network (GIIN), impact investing, which is on the rise, is described as making investments with the intention of generating positive and measurable social and environmental impact alongside a financial return. Depending on the investor's goals, the return expectations of impact investments range from below-market rate to market-rate returns (GIIN, 2020). The GIIN estimates the current size of the global impact investing market to be $502 billion, with the USA and Canada having the highest share of assets under management (AUM) by region and sub-Saharan Africa ranking fourth (Hand et al., 2020). Yet, the CCIs remain overlooked by traditional financial institutions and impact investors. In 2020, a GIIN report showed that 0% of impact investment is deployed in the arts and culture sector (Hand et al., 2020). To date, social finance has stayed away from investing in the CCIs and has not taken the time to really understand its needs.

However, this is beginning to change. In November 2019 the United Nations declared 2021 the International Year of Creative Economy for Sustainable Development, highlighting the role that the CCIs hold to achieve the Sustainable Development Goals (SDGs) and the 2030 Agenda (UN, 2019). In July 2020, Upstart Co-Lab (a US-based creative-social finance intermediary) launched a Member Community that committed to investing $1 billion to fund impact investments in artists and enterprises that can address social problems in creative ways.

Finance for CCIs in Africa: policy gaps and international networks

Africa represents an interesting context to explore the potential of CCIs, policy initiatives and intermediaries (Comunian et al., 2021). And in particular, Kenya and East Africa have led many international development strategies for CCIs. The CCIs in East Africa have long benefited from programmes run by developmental financial institutions, charitable organisations and philanthropic funds. In Kenya, arts organisations and programmes have received grants from institutions like the British Council, Goethe-Institut and French Cultural Centre as well as funders like Hivos and Forum Civ, among others. These foreign grants have been used to support the launch and survival of many of the better-known creative ventures that exist in Kenya today. Organisations like GoDown (also discussed in Chapter 7), Kuona and Kwani benefited from these foreign investments to support local networks, honing talent and subsidising the cost of doing business (Mawazo Institute, 2019). However, with the shift of aid to trade, the availability of these grants decreased and they became highly competitive. In addition, the grant model was not a sustainable source of investment for cultural organisations.

Against this backdrop, HEVA fund has established new models of financing and supporting the sector. In 2014, HEVA received support from Hivos to launch its first fund, an early-stage fund to invest in businesses in fashion and apparel, crafts and handmade items, film production and photography as well as live music and events. This was the first time commercial models were used to invest in creative businesses by a private fund. In 2018, HEVA and Agence Française de Développement (AFD) signed a credit facility agreement to support the funds' expansion as well as a technical assistance agreement for capacity and skills building. This was the first time such an agreement had been signed in the sector.

Creative industry finance: HEVA fund

Initial steps and scope of action

Founded in 2012, the Nest Collective[2] is a multidisciplinary arts organisation in Kenya that uses a holistic applied-research methodology to create cultural bodies of work with film, fashion, literature and other media. These interventions are designed to engage audiences using multiple points of entry and reflection, while also advancing the aesthetic and artistic value. The Nest's work usually finds multiple platforms, spaces and audiences, including academia, other cultural practitioners, civil society, young people in urban spaces, and through numerous forms of media. The Nest's work, born in Nairobi, makes strong references to African urban and contemporary experiences and their work continues to draw on histories and reflections about possible futures.

The Nest had for a period of time been inquiring about artistic livelihoods, and what would need to be done to ensure that artists were able to live sustainably from their art. In 2013, the Nest Collective commissioned a feasibility study on the creative economy in East Africa. This research was supported by Hivos East Africa[3], an organisation founded in 1968, inspired by humanist values and whose work and interventions in the Kenyan CCIs had been instrumental in the growth of the CCIs.

While there was existing research, it did not address questions surrounding finance, including viable and sustainable solutions to fund creative entrepreneurs through investment tools such as loans and equity. The Nest had proposed a debt guarantee fund for the creative sector and this study would determine whether or not a guarantee fund was the best solution to address the challenges creative entrepreneurs face when seeking financing. The scope of this feasibility study included mapping out challenges faced by creative entrepreneurs, attitudes towards financing options, a survey of interventions in place to address challenges faced by the creative sector in other parts of the world, as well as the experience and appetite of formal financial institutions for working with guarantee funds. Discussions with financial institutions revealed they had not sufficiently interacted with the CCIs and perceived it as being a high-risk sector due to the intangible nature of art coupled with a lack of understanding of art by both financial institutions and the general public. The key findings highlighted were: a lack of public appreciation for art; inadequate business skills; lack of market access; a lack of exhibition spaces, financing and expensive equipment.

For the CCIs to thrive, a lot more than financial investment was needed. There was a clear gap in policy, especially when it came to the ecosystem. In addition, there was not enough data to support investment into the CCIs by governments and private investors. This meant that a key intervention needed would be research and policy work to inform and build a favourable business environment. Secondly, investors needed to structure more favourable financial products that considered the context of the entrepreneurs in the CCIs. The needs of youth needed to be considered, including the barriers to accessing finance and implementing financing models. Business and technical training were also limited. Finally, there was a need for the public and private sectors and developmental organisations to work together in providing support for the sector at various levels.

As a result, HEVA fund was created. It aimed to bring together an accelerator programme, an online portal and an equity guarantee fund (Figure 4.1) to create a holistic approach towards finance and support for CCIs in Kenya and East Africa.

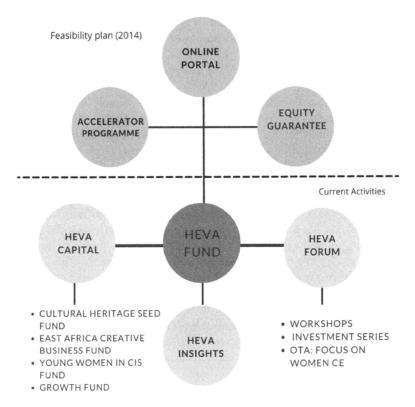

Figure 4.1 HEVA fund: from feasibility to current activities.
Note: CE, creative enterprise; CIS, creative industries.

HEVA fund: a holistic approach

In 2014, HEVA rolled out an early-stage fund, designed to respond to these constraints. Since then, HEVA has actively made investments in 50 businesses (outlined below) from various sub-sectors in CCIs, worked to publish data and several reports (listed in Table 4.1) and trained more than 8,000 entrepreneurs in business and technical skills. HEVA also influenced policy conversations around ease of doing business for CCIs.

In 2016, HEVA hosted the National Creative Economy Dialogues, an official side event to the United Nations Conference on Trade and Development (UNCTAD) 14th Global Conference. The symposium explored questions around strategic public investment policies,

Table 4.1 List of reports developed by HEVA (2017–2020)

Impact of COVID-19 Pandemic on Kenya's Creative Industries: Creative Industry Options and Strategies (2020)	HEVA sought to understand the impact of the novel coronavirus pandemic through a needs-analysis exercise, which generated responses from creative and cultural industry practitioners, policy experts and sector representation organisations throughout Kenya, Uganda, Tanzania and Rwanda
Youth and Employment Advisory (2020)	In January 2020, the Royal Danish Embassy commissioned HEVA to carry out a study in Kenya to review the country's youth-related engagements, in order to inform Denmark's engagement with Kenya to support the government and the population of Kenya to implement Vision 2030, and contribute to achieving selected UN Sustainable Development Goals in Kenya
Uhuru Market Center of Excellence Action Research (2019)	In line with the Big Four Agenda, the government of Kenya commissioned HEVA to carry out action research of Uhuru Market, the government-commissioned HEVA fund, which, in collaboration with the Executive Office of the President, would conduct an action research project with the aim of helping producers reduce inefficiencies, increase value addition, increase value chain integration and grow the product markets. This was in line with the Big Four Agenda of creating sustainable jobs and reducing over-reliance on imported garments, especially second-hand clothing and shoes (Mitumba), approximated at 100,000 tonnes annually in order to address the competitiveness constraints in the garment and textiles value chains
Feasibility Study of Garment Manufacturing and Retail in Kenya (2017)	In line with the ambitions to support competitiveness in the garment-manufacturing sector for domestic following, HEVA initiated consultations with the Executive Office of the President as well as United Nations Industrial Development Organization's (UNIDO's) Global Ambassador Dr Helen Hai, HEVA, with the aim of generating insights to establish a national fashion and garments strategy. The aims of this study were: - To understand the factors limiting cost-competitiveness of locally produced garments - To determine the feasibility of setting up a manufacturing unit for local design production targeting the domestic market

(*continued*)

Table 4.1 Cont.

	- To understand the Kenyan fashion retail market and consumer habits
Fashion, Textiles and Apparel Value Chains Scoping (2017)	In 2017, HEVA undertook scoping visits in Rwanda and Ethiopia to get a deeper understanding of the sector in both countries with the aim of strengthening manufacturing and retail networks while looking into possible collaboration and investment opportunities
Ease of Doing Business Reports (2017)	The British Council commissioned HEVA fund to review and finalise the Creative Economy Business Environment Reform Facility (BERF) Report (Kennedy Manyala, October 2016), with the following aims: • Consider the 2016 report in order to make recommendations for review as well as to define the scope for this review process • Identify and investigate the critical business environment questions for the creative sector in Kenya, in the immediate and long term • Explore the specific role of government in ensuring the sustainability of the creative sector in Kenya

sustainable philanthropic and developmental finance approaches as well as thriving private capital and effective corporate partnerships.

Today the activities of HEVA fund can be articulated under three main headings:

1. *HEVA capital* consists of the three funds designed to catalyse the growth strategies of early-stage ventures, optimise creative-sector value chains and provide working capital and cash flow solutions as well as a growth fund which offers follow-on financing, matching fund and guarantees for creative-sector enterprises.
2. *HEVA forum* curates a dynamic mix of tailored one-on-one consulting opportunities and specialised skills-building workshops along with peer learning opportunities. These learning programmes are necessary to inspire creative professionals to innovate their ideas and design processes, improve their production and business models, help rethink their product life cycles, help to adopt low-environmental-impact materials, minimising waste and increase the unit value of their products – which can satisfy and fulfil the needs of targeted market segments.

3. *HEVA insights* includes data collection and publishing of reports that go deeper into CCI value chains, ease of doing business, budget analysis and engaging with government and policymakers to ensure the sector's needs are well presented. The lack of data in this sector has been named a major challenge for government and other stakeholders in creating programmes and policies for CCIs. HEVA uses data-driven methodologies and analysis to assess the value of the CCI ecosystem, identify growth areas, and produce strategies that deliver measurable economic and social benefits. Through this approach it has contributed to the development of favourable laws and regulations, including the Film Policy (2017), Kenya Cultural Centre Policy (2018), Culture Bill (2016), the formation of the Arts, Social Welfare and Sports Fund (2018), the Copyrights Act (amendment, 2019), the Reduction on Import Duties on finished products (2019), among others.

Investing in CCIs: facilities, lessons learnt and case studies

Over the seven years HEVA has been operating, it has offered financial products that are tailored to the sector's needs. The traditional financial institutions used a one-size-fits all approach. For example, a fashion company with fluctuating seasonal sales might not qualify for a traditional term loan because its revenues might seem too varied – even though that is the nature of the sector. HEVA has developed specific financial products to respond to the needs of the sector. These include HEVA's innovative revenue share, lease-to-own models, line of credit and convertible debt models, which do not affect the beneficiary's business cash flow when making payments. Alongside the finance facility, businesses benefit from enterprise and skills-building interventions.

A HEVA facility is usually given to a business after a rigorous evaluation process that includes a creative committee, business committee, pitch session, due diligence and financial modelling. Importantly, this is also a collaborative process that allows the entrepreneur to have deeper insights into the growth trajectory of its company and work hand in hand with the team. This process is the first level of business support.

At the creative committee stage, the product's aesthetics and viability are measured against the target market by a team of industry experts. Feedback at this level is very insightful to entrepreneurs as they can see whether there is a proper market–product fit. At the pitch panel, the entrepreneurs and their team get to interact with the industry experts directly. The panel is made up of both industry/sectoral experts and business development experts. The due-diligence stage ensures that the company is compliant with all the legal, business and tax frameworks. If not, then suggestions are made about how they can comply and often the fund has included this as a post-investment business support component.

The final stage is the financial modelling stage, where a company's historical financial performance is used to forecast future earnings. The models are co-created with the entrepreneurs to ensure that their aspirations for their businesses are well captured and own the output. The process in itself is structured so that it is the first level of business support for participants, and any business that goes through it gains value.

The composition of the fund's board has also largely contributed to the success of HEVA's interventions. Decisions made on investments and how to engage with the sector are influenced by the decisions made by HEVA's board, some of whom are creative practitioners and, unlike traditional funders, understand the challenges from first-hand experience.

In a space that has been characterised by substantial ticket sizes for investments, HEVA has focused on providing tailored financial investments for dynamic CCIs. The fund considers lower ticket sizes in the seed and early-stage funds up to 30,000, to mid-level tickets of $50,000–$100,000. HEVA has three central funds through which it invests in businesses: (1) seed stage; (2) young women in CCIs; and (3) growth fund.

Seed stage: cultural heritage seed fund

HEVA established a short-term seed fund facility looking to support and stimulate culture and heritage start-ups in Kenya, collaborating with the British Council. This fund was intended to create inclusive development, by working directly in the areas of music, film, fashion, crafts, gaming and performing arts, as well as tourism projects which celebrate and preserve heritage. The fund used hybrid grant and loan facilities. Grants were used to cushion the early-stage businesses and produce and offset some running costs, and the loans went toward direct production costs and purchase of equipment. An example of business supported by this fund is Paukwa House, a storytelling firm created to infuse Kenyan national narratives with positive fact-based stories. Through storytelling, they aim to show a side of Kenya that Kenyans can be proud of. HEVA's investment went towards the production of their content campaigns, as well as to business development in order to increase their revenue potential.

Young women in CCIs

HEVA designed a facility aimed at young women in CCIs, focusing on early-stage financing and business support to exclusively support women-owned and women-led early-stage enterprises in Kenya, in collaboration with JENGA CCI, a project of the Goethe-Institut Kenya and GIZ[4]. This facility was directed at supporting the businesses' working capital needs and acquisition of production assets. An example of a company HEVA invested in under this facility is Peperuka, an apparel brand that enriches the Kenyan cultural experience by using colloquialisms, historical figures and inspirational pan-African icons as muses for the charming, vibrant and varied products. Through this investment, Peperuka expanded its distribution network and increased its available working capital.

Growth fund

In 2018, HEVA signed an agreement with the AFD (French Development Agency) to expand its investments into growth-stage businesses. The fund was designed to provide follow-on growth financing to more mature ventures. It invested in reducing supply-side constraints, addressing information asymmetry, increasing market linkages and driving co-investments with other commercial finance providers. In 2020, HEVA expanded this facility to East Africa businesses, particularly Rwanda, Uganda, Tanzania and Ethiopia. Under this scheme, Mookh Africa, a social-eCommerce platform that allows sellers to quickly and easily set up online stores with installed payment integration, was funded. The platform comprises of fintech solution building digital solutions for African small–medium enterprises (SMEs) and their global customers.

OTA: HEVA's programmatic focus on women in CCIs

Women (often young) creative practitioners are making a mark in the CCIs internationally. While this development is exciting, the businesses operate in an unfavourable environment which significantly limits the growth potential. It is also disproportionately difficult for young women entrepreneurs. They usually face numerous cultural and gender barriers which further complicate business ownership. They also struggle to access growth finance: according to Morton et al. (2014), women are less likely than men to have access to formal banking and commercial finance. In 2019, HEVA launched OTA, a programmatic focus on women in CCIs, set up to build the competitiveness and sustainability of women-owned and women-led businesses. The focus was informed by the analysis of

HEVA's baseline studies, which showed the significant involvement and impact of women in the fast-growing creative enterprises in the region, mirroring that on the rest of the African continent as well as in the world. The programme both addresses access to credit challenges as well as gives a platform for women entrepreneurs to access capacity building, business support and mentorship opportunities.

Conclusions

This chapter contributes to our knowledge of the importance of finance for CCI development in Africa, building on previous reflections by Mokuolu et al. (2021) but adding more specific reflection in the context of Kenya and East Africa. The case study of HEVA fund allowed us to reflect on the importance of new funding and finance frameworks for CCIs in Africa. It has also highlighted the development opportunities for intermediaries and initiatives addressing CCI finance to improve the economic and socio-cultural impact of CCIs. Furthermore, it provided an in-depth reflection on how creative intermediaries develop support initiatives from feasibility to delivery. It also provided critical learning on the importance of integrating a range of activities, not just finance but also training and skills development.

The chapter put forward three key findings. Firstly, effective financing for the CCIs requires specific knowledge and understanding of CCIs. Intermediaries working and supporting the sector – like HEVA – are better placed than generic financial institutions in supporting CCI entrepreneurs and meeting their needs. Secondly, within the sector, it is important to consider the importance of finance and development support for CCIs as integrated because finance underpins cash flow but also skill development and the aims of entrepreneurs which often extend beyond profit and growth. Finally, CCI finance needs to grow with the support of policy frameworks and national and international financial institutions and partners. National governments must create opportunities for these networks and collaborations to develop. CCIs in Africa are still in the early growth stages, which means that there is a need for public and private partnerships to support their further development. In particular, the government's role is to ensure that policies foster the sector's growth and to support investment in extensive infrastructure and skills development. The private sector's role should be in providing innovative finance to these businesses to fuel their growth.

Although this chapter provided an initial reflection on the development of CCI finance in East Africa, more research is needed to consider how additional creative intermediaries can be supported to develop similar facilities across Africa. While HEVA is already exploring interventions and collaborations beyond East Africa, the challenges of different policy frameworks, financial mechanisms and markets across Africa's different regions and nations make knowledge sharing and joint development a challenge. More research is needed to consider how finance for CCIs can become a priority and cornerstone of CCI development across the continent.

Notes

1 A contract with the public sector, whereby it pays for social outcomes and passes on the part of the savings achieved to investors.
2 For more information about the Nest Collective, see www.thisisthenest.com/about (accessed 4th January 2021).
3 For more information on the work of Hivos, see https://east-africa.hivos.org/who-we-are/ (accessed 4th January 2021).
4 For more information, see www.goethe.de/ins/ke/en/kul/sup/cci.html (accessed 4th January 2021).

References

ACEVO (2010) *Understanding Social Investment*. London: Association of Chief Executives of Voluntary Organisations (ACEVO).
Caves, R. E. (2000) *Creative Industries: Contracts between Art and Commerce*. Revised 2nd edn. Cambridge: Harvard University Press.
Comunian, R., England, L. and Hracs, B. J. (2022) Cultural intermediaries revisited: lessons from Cape Town, Nairobi and Lagos. In: Hracs, B. J., Brydges, T., Haisch, T., Hauge, A., Jansson, J. and Sjöholm, J. (eds.) *Culture, Creativity and Economy: Collaborative Practices, Value Creation and Spaces of Creativity*. London: Routledge.
Creative United (2018) *Social Impact Report: The Financialization of Social Impact in the Cultural Economy and Creative Industries in the UK*. London: Creative United.
Dümcke, C., Jaurová, Z. and Inkei, P. (2014) *Opportunities for CCSs to Access Finance in the EU – Short Analytical Report*. Available at: www.interarts.net/descargas/interarts2574.pdf (accessed 9 June 2018).
European Commission (2013) *Survey on Access to Finance for Cultural and Creative Sectors*. Available at: http://ec.europa.eu/assets/eac/culture/library/studies/access-finance_en.pdf (accessed 9 June 2018).
GIIN (2020) *What You Need to Know About Impact Investing, GIIN*. Available at: https://thegiin.org/impact-investing/need-to-know/#s2Study/05Kenya_GIIN_eastafrica_DIGITAL.pdf (accessed 15 August 2020).
Hand, D. et al. (2020) *GIIN Annual Impact Investor Survey* (10th edn). *Global Impact Investment Network (GIIN)*. Available at: https://thegiin.org/assets/GIIN Annual Impact Investor Survey 2020.pdf (accessed 9 June 2018).

Hracs, B. J. (2015) Cultural intermediaries in the digital age: the case of independent musicians and managers in Toronto. *Regional Studies*, 49(3): 461–475.

Kenny, B. (2015) *Philanthropy 2.0: Investing with a Purpose.* Available at: www.hbs.edu/news/articles/Pages/philanthropy-2.0.aspx (accessed 10 November 2017).

Mawazo Institute (2019) *Nairobi Ideas Exchange: Report on Investing in Kenya's Creative Economy.* Available at: https://static1.squarespace.com/static/57d0650220099eacd505d3fc/t/5e500309097a363847b6790d/1582302049299/NIExchange_Investing+in+Arts+Report+%28Feb+2020%29.pdf (accessed 10 December 2020).

Mokuolu, Y., Kay, V. and Velilla-Zuloaga, C. M. (2021) Higher education and policy for creative economies in Africa. In: Comunian, R., Hracs, B. J. and England, L., (eds) *Higher Education and Policy for Creative Economies in Africa.* London: Routledge, pp. 113–130.

Monclus, R. P. (2015) Public banking for the cultural sector: financial instruments and the new financial intermediaries. *International Review of Social Research*, 5(2): 88–101.

Morton, M., Klugman, J., Hanmer, L. and Singer, D. (2014) *Gender at Work: A Companion to the World Development Report on Jobs.* Washington, DC: World Bank Group.

NESTA (2018) Repayable finance in the arts and cultural sector. London: NESTA. Available at: https://media.nesta.org.uk/documents/repayable-finance-arts-cultural-sector.pdf (accessed 10 December 2020).

Nguyen, P. (2020) More than art – grants beyond creative industries. *Creative Vitality Suite.* Available at: https://cvsuite.org/2017/07/10/art-grants-beyond-creative-industries/ (accessed 9 June 2018).

Phills Jr, J. A., Deiglmeier, K. and Miller, D. T. (2008) Rediscovering social innovation. *Stanford Social Innovation Review*, Fall, 6(4):34–43.

UN (2019) *United Nations – Declaration: 2021 as International Year of Creative Economy for Sustainable Development.* New York: United Nations Publications. Available at: https://undocs.org/A/C.2/74/L.16/Rev.1 (accessed 10 December 2020).

UNESCO (2015) *Post-2015 Dialogues on Culture and Development.* Available at: https://unesdoc.unesco.org/ark:/48223/pf0000232266 (accessed 9 June 2020).

Upstart Co-lab (2017) *A Creativity Lens for Impact Investing.* New York: Upstart Co-lab.

Vogel, H. L. (2010) *Entertainment Industry Economics: A Guide for Financial Analysis*, 8th edn. Cambridge: Cambridge University Press.

5 Creative coworking in Nigeria

Emerging trends, opportunities and future scenarios

Damilola Adegoke and Roberta Comunian

Introduction

There has been growing attention in the creative economy literature on opportunities and dynamics offered by coworking. More than a decade after the term started to emerge (Moriset, 2013), the concept is now increasingly popular globally. Gandini et al. (2017) have discussed the emergence of coworking in western societies as a response to flexibilisation and casualisation of work, especially in the aftermath of the global financial crisis in 2008. However, the social realities and processes of coworking spaces in developing countries are still absent or are yet to be adequately captured by literature. This chapter explores whether some of these considerations might also be valid in developing countries, with a specific focus on Nigeria. Looking at an economically booming African country like Nigeria provides new and valuable insights from a non-western (Alacovska and Gill, 2019) view of creative coworking. This context also responds to a different economic and policy trajectory from the usual coworking contexts. New coworking spaces have opened up in the country, led by various stakeholders (from universities to private investors). The chapter aims to map the phenomenon and provide an initial understanding of the way these spaces emerge in developing countries and what different needs and challenges are present in emerging economies.

The chapter begins by reviewing the literature on coworking, with a specific focus on research in the African context and Nigeria. Using Google Trends analysis data, we then show the growing interest in coworking in Nigeria and specifically Lagos and Abuja. Here, we also use desktop research and primary data collected via an online survey to look at the business model of coworking spaces in Nigeria, highlighting the growth dynamics of the sector and the challenges it faces. Finally, we highlight the factors that may have influenced the fast growth of

DOI: 10.4324/9781003191681-5

coworking in Nigeria and draw conclusions on the results and give directions for future research.

Creative coworking: global trends

The idea of coworking emerged in America and Europe in the past decade in response to new emerging work patterns of work, mainly in the creative and digital economy, but also due to inner urban spaces becoming available and the need for investment (Sargent and Daniels, 2016). Moriset (2013) reports data from Deskwanted (a portal committed to coworking) in 2013 listing 2500 coworking spaces established in 80 countries across the globe. A similar global platform, identified in 2019, confirmed and verified 9452 coworking spaces globally. Many factors can explain this exponential growth. Firstly, the numbers of creative workers and in turn the creative economy have grown globally (UNCTAD, 2018). Secondly, many established companies started outsourcing jobs in response to economic pressure and the 2008 global financial crisis. The precarity of creative work internationally has meant a growth in freelancers (Comunian and England, 2020). However, as Moriset (2013) highlights, it also connects with the increase in urban start-ups and entrepreneurs, who want to take full advantage of business opportunities and possible collaboration with others. In fact, coworking spaces are places primarily designed for hosting and social working, especially among entrepreneurs who engage in creative business ideas and aspire to communicating these ideas with others (Moriset, 2013).

A coworking space is a shared work setting that allows small business individuals from diverse fields of work and knowledge to carry out their business activities autonomously and/or collectively within a collaborative business environment. This includes shared facilities to defray running and operational costs that would otherwise be borne by individual small businesses (Spinuzzi, 2012). This cooperative model is attractive to budding entrepreneurs in developing societies with limited access to needed facilities. In recent times, studies in African contexts have highlighted the value of the informal learning environment, idea generation and innovation (Kelly and Firestone, 2016; Akanle and Omotayo, 2020; Comunian and Jacobi, 2021).

Research on coworking also highlights their connection with Oldenburg's (1989) idea of "third spaces": places different from home and work settings in which people regularly gather, share ideas and mingle in a free, informal manner. Scholars have found that an informal environment positively impacts social interaction, networking, social ties and collaboration among people from different backgrounds (McLaughlin and Faulkner, 2012; Spinuzzi, 2012). These spaces offer people opportunities to learn from one another through social interaction and collaboration (Bilandzic and Foth, 2013; Lumley, 2014). It is a space for creative individuals to exchange ideas in a more relaxing environment, among peers passing through the same phase and experiencing the same challenges, far away from the tasking social, political, economic and securing concerns surrounding them. Core value expectations and commitments such as association, openness, community, accessibility and sustainability are essential criteria for participation in these spaces (Bates, 2011; Bouncken et al., 2018).

Coworking, incubation and acceleration spaces

In order to better understand the roles and objectives of coworking spaces in contemporary society, it is essential to explore the relationship between incubation spaces, coworking spaces, technology hubs and acceleration spaces (Kojo and Nenonen, 2016). Coworking spaces differ from telecentres, flexible office facilities and other forms of incubators and start-up accelerators. Telecentres are drop-in offices with a low level of professional interactions among co-actors; flexible office facilities are mainly office rental solutions that do not attempt to create any form of cooperative practice or entrepreneurial hub among individuals; while incubators are essentially devoted to start-up projects or schemes. Building on the work of Schmidt et al. (2014) and Fuzi (2015), we highlight that, in coworking spaces, the focus is merely on providing shared facilities and facilitating the work of freelancers. In the case of incubation spaces, instead, a series of programmes is designed and deployed to support start-ups and develop new products or services. Incubation spaces are also equipped with instruments and programmes to help business individuals and professionals, from mentoring to finance. Coworking spaces tend to be more conducive to the business of a range of creative freelancers, while incubation spaces tend to target more companies in the area of information and communications technology (ICT) and digital. Furthermore, accelerators connect more strongly with a framework of financial support, like business angels and small-scale individual investors, that enable companies to start on a quick path of development (Clarysse et al., 2015).

In the case of Nigeria, incubation spaces can also help tackle social and economic issues like unemployment, poverty and low revenue generation (Akanle and Omotayo, 2020) by giving access to shared resources and possibilities to a range of different members of the community.

Space is not just physical but also enables social networking activities and partnerships. This can facilitate socio-economic development and knowledge building among individuals or organisations. Hence, it is possible to have a group of business individuals and professionals in space/place working together to achieve greater efficiency, innovation and inclusion on a project through mutual interaction.

Therefore, it is essential to consider the notion of the coworking space as a continuum of "third spaces" that have emerged recently to address a range of workers' and business needs (Weijs-Perrée et al., 2019), from tech hub, entrepreneur centres and innovation spaces. These emerging business concepts have encouraged new ideas, job opportunities and social formation in many African countries (Friederici, 2018). The establishment of coworking spaces in some of Africa's urban centres is influenced by changes in population, organisational goals, business structure, entrepreneurial skill, technology and international relations. Many African coworking spaces are also sponsored or co-sponsored by international governmental and non-governmental organisations such as the World Bank and World Wide Web Foundation (Kelly and Firestone, 2016). However, in recent times, local business organisations and educational institutions have begun to replicate this idea.

Coworking spaces in Nigeria: from the past to the present

Much of the international literature seems to highlight the coworking model's success and diffusion as the mere international expansion from the Global North to the rest of the world (Luo and Chan, 2020). However, our research considers how the growth of Nigerian coworking spaces seems to connect with other societal characteristics of the country.

The idea of coworking spaces is not entirely new to Nigeria. Before the country's independence from colonial rule, studies (Omobowale and Omobowale, 2019) have shown that a significant number of Nigerians in both rural and urban areas participate in some form of informal cooperative workspaces. This is historically reflected in the *aro* and *owe* labour-trading system of the Yoruba people of southwest Nigeria (Fadipẹ et al., 1970; Agiri, 1983). In the northern region of the country, the Hausa and Nupe continue to have similar forms of cooperative labour, including communal farm labour, exchange farm labour and bonded labour. In the southwestern part of the country, Igbo people practised a reciprocal labour exchange system known as *igba-onwo-oru* between people of an age grade tied by marriage and kinship (Mbakwe, 2015).

The concept of cooperative workspaces is common in developing societies due to several economic limitations and other sociocultural considerations, not only in Nigeria. In many African societies, there is a shared cultural belief that informal and formal spaces should be jointly utilised among different stakeholders. This is specifically true if the shared space is used to improve the community's socio-economic conditions (Wanyama, 2009). There are community lands and markets; these shared spaces provide opportunities for shared experiences and information, not only shared geographical spaces. The various guilds (Yakubu, 2002), such as the various guilds of hunters and textile women workers spread across Yoruba region, the guild of bronzesmiths in Benin and the herbalist guilds in Nupe land, exemplify this. All these various trades comprise members who collectively work together in shared spaces. For example, looking at the famous tradition of Adire in Abeokuta, it is common to find local women engaged in the creative textile industry using shared facilities for their trade. This helps spread risks, costs and opportunities (Bakare and Kolawole, 2019).

The underlying philosophy is captured in several Yoruba (one of the dominant ethnic groups in Nigeria) aphorisms and proverbs such as: "*Ka rin ka po, yiye ni yeni*", translated as "walking together in a team or group is more befitting than walking alone"; others include: "*Ka jose po, kajola*", meaning "shared work equals shared prosperity"; "*Enìkan kì í je, kí ìlú fè*", which is "the prosperity of a single person does not translate to that of his community", "*Ajoje ko dun bi enikan koni*", translated as "there is joy in shared prosperity". The social interpretation of these indigenous views highlights the prominence of the concept of communal labour and coworking spaces amongst indigenous people and also shows that the concept is not alien to the country (Adebayo and Olonisakin, 2018).

The modern take on this concept of coworking is gaining prominence in contemporary Nigeria, because of the challenge for small business owners and budding professionals to take on the costs of running office spaces together with the attendant costs of maintaining such spaces in a developing society (Okpara and Kabongo, 2009). There is also the issue of paucity of spaces given urban overpopulation in the commercial cities of the country, specifically Lagos (Barredo and Demicheli, 2003). These realities warrant the adoption of a new approach to mitigating these challenges. Also, coworking is inspired by essential benefits and supports (i.e. free internet services, coffee and mentorship) that members enjoy, especially those who are new in their professional career or line of business.

In Nigerian urban areas, coworking spaces are perceived as informal settings, where individuals from diverse fields of work and knowledge interrelate with one another to learn new ideas and ways to carry out business activities autonomously and/or collectively. Unlike traditional coworking spaces, modern-day coworking spaces perform a wide range of services to members or subscribers depending on the objectives of each coworking space (Akanle and Omotayo, 2020).

Coworking in Africa and Nigeria: data on expansion and business models

Social workplaces, experts in the coworking industry and organisers of the oldest coworking conference worldwide estimated the number of coworking spaces in Africa grew from about 24 spaces in 2013 to over 250 spaces in 2016. The most recent report (2019) from Coworking Insights talks about 381 coworking spaces in Africa, while Coworker. com lists 633.[1] The sector's data and growth are in continuous evolution, but the growing trends in Africa seem to confirm a push towards this form of working and business development.

While these numbers confirm a growing phenomenon, little attention has been paid to the study of coworking spaces in contemporary Africa, and in Nigeria specifically, in academic literature. A careful browse of literature in academic databases such as Google Scholar, Scopus and Web of Science reveals this absence (Akanle and Omotayo, 2020). The term is gaining gradual ascendancy in both media and academic discourses, partly due to increased internet access and affordability. A Google Trend[2] analysis (Jun et al., 2018) of the term "coworking spaces" in Nigeria compared with worldwide usage of the term from 2004 to 2019 showed a steady steep rise globally in the early 2000s and a rapid increase from late 2010s for Nigeria, as shown in Figure 5.1.

If we focus specifically on Nigeria, we can compare two datasets. The November 2017 report from Venia seems to provide a more detailed listing of coworking in Nigeria geographically, including email addresses of all providers. Looking at the more recent database listing of Coworkers.com (July 2020) we can see how even in the space of two years the numbers have grown. However, the intensity of presence remains very similar, with Lagos, considered the economic capital of Nigeria, hosting between 68.4% and 65.8% of the coworking spaces, Abuja, the formal and political capital between 13.2% and 16.9% and other locations only having a minor presence (Table 5.1).

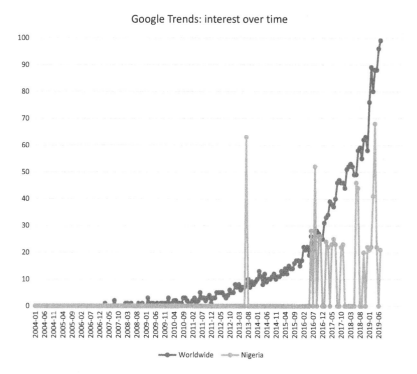

Figure 5.1 Google Trends for the term "coworking space" in Nigeria and worldwide between 2004 and 2019.

Coworkers.com allows us to reflect on the services offered by the providers. Of the 136 offering desk working space, 104 also offer private offices and 114 offer the service of renting meeting rooms. Almost all provide some basic services as high-speed internet and air conditioning are offered by 120 out of 136. However, if we look at more specialised business services the provision is much more reduced (Table 5.2). For example, in relation to supporting workers and businesses, 47.1% of the providers offer some form of workshop activities, but only 32.4 % provide mentorship programmes. If we look at the more social or networking services, while 68.4% provide events, only 19.1% create a Facebook group (and fewer invest in an app) to support interaction amongst members.

Using the list of coworking spaces identified by Venia (2017) in Nigeria and their contact details, we were able to contact via email a total of 76 creative coworking hubs in Nigeria; we asked them to complete

Table 5.1 Number of working spaces in Nigeria

Location	Coworker.com (July 2020)	Venia Report (Nov. 2017)
Lagos (incl. Lekki, Ikeja)	94 (68.4 %)	50 (65.8%)
Abuja	23 (16.9%)	10 (13.2%)
Rivers (Port Harcourt)	5 (3.7%)	4 (5.3%)
Oyo (Ibadan)	5 (3.7%)	3 (3.9%)
Kwara (Ilorin)	2 (1.5%)	1 (1.3%)
Enugu State (Enugu)	2 (1.5%)	0
Ogun (Ogun)	0	2 (2.6%)
Akwa-Ibom (Uyo)	0	2 (2.6%)
Delta (Warri and Asaba)	1 (0.7%)	1 (1.3%)
Plateau (Jos)	1 (0.7%)	1 (1.3%)
Imo State (Owerri)	1 (0.7%)	1 (1.3%)
Benin City	1 (0.7%)	1 (1.3%)
Bayelsa State (Yenagoa)	1 (0.7%)	0
Kaduna	1 (0.7%)	1 (1.3%)
Imo State	1 (0.7%)	
Kano	0	1 (1.3%)
Total	**136**	**76**

Source: Co-worker.com and Nigeria coworking report (Venia, 2017).

Table 5.2 Services provided by the 136 coworking spaces in Nigeria

Out of 136 providers	Number of providers (out of 136) and percentage
Business services	
Workshops	64 (47.1%)
Mentorship programme	44 (32.4%)
Incubators programme	37 (27.2%)
Accelerator programme	35 (25.7%)
Social and networking	
Events	93 (68.4%)
Facebook group for members	26 (19.1%)
Slack channel for members	19 (14%)
Community app	23 (16.9%)
Community drinks	27 (19.9%)
Community lunches	25 (18.4%)

a brief survey. The survey inquired about their location, business structure and primary business model but also included questions about the challenges faced by coworking in Nigeria. The survey received a 19.7% return rate (15 completed surveys). Although this is overall a low response rate[3] and does not have specific statistical significance, it still provides some further insights on the coworking sector in Nigeria.

All respondents identified themselves in the survey as *coworking spaces* (mainly for freelancers, workers and small companies to run business). However, 11 of them also identified with the tag of *incubators* (supporting start-up businesses) and ten with the role of *tech hub* and *innovation lab* (focusing on new-ideas generation) while two also identified themselves with the role of *accelerator* (investing in the companies and their growth). This highlights, as discussed previously, that the role and functions of coworking spaces are not only to provide space to work but also to support new businesses and new ideas to develop. The data on the business models with which the respondents identified were also fascinating. Out of the 15 respondents, 11 spaces were privately owned by individuals (nine) and with investors (two). Two combined private ownership with a not-for-profit business model and one identified uniquely as not for profit. The last one was formed via a private–public partnership (PPP) model (Figure 5.2).

Supporting the trend we discussed above on the growing number of coworking spaces forecasted globally, 73% of the respondents stated that demand and their business were growing,[4] while 3.2% considered the forecast to be stable (Figure 5.3). Only one respondent did not reply as they stated they had to temporarily close to re-think their business model.

The survey also asked about the main challenges experienced by coworking spaces in Nigeria. The main challenges (listed in Table 5.3) are infrastructural. For half of the respondents, these include the need

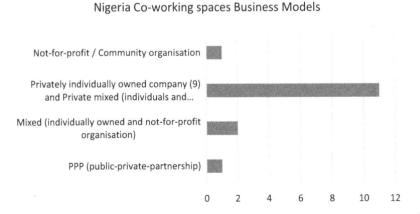

Figure 5.2 Nigeria coworking spaces business models.

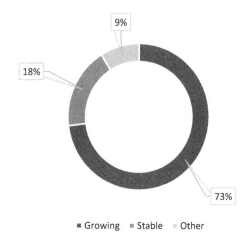

Figure 5.3 Coworking as a growing business in Nigeria.

Table 5.3 Challenges faced by coworking spaces in Nigeria

Challenges experienced	Number of responses
Power	7
Internet connectivity	7
Access to funds/support	6
Policies/government support	5
Costs of infrastructure	5
Awareness	2
Intellectual property infringement regulation	2
Access to skills	1

for power and internet connectivity to be made more steadily available across the country. The lack of funding and support from the government were considered challenges for a third of the respondents.

Promoting of coworking spaces in Nigeria: enablers and policy needs

Several factors account for the expansion of coworking spaces in contemporary Nigeria. These factors fall under four broad categories: economic, socio-psychological, environmental and technological.

Firstly, the decision to engage in coworking spaces is typically informed by *economic factors* and calculations of cost–benefit analysis. In consideration of these economic benefits, a large number of people (especially professionals, students and entrepreneurs) opt to work in coworking spaces instead of going it all alone. The economic factors such as financial cost, job opportunities and the income derived from engaging in coworking spaces are motivating and determining variables. These variables influence the decision to invest in the setting-up of coworking spaces and the decision to participate in the coworking spaces. From our data, it is possible to read how the private sector sees this as a sector of expansion – especially in response to the rise in population and youth entering the labour market – and worthy of investment.

Similarly, the decision to engage in coworking spaces could be due to social and psychological conditions such as the sensory environment, sense of belonging and cognitive symbols. These *socio-psychological factors* predispose people to utilise coworking spaces and facilities (Bates, 2011). In Nigeria and perhaps other African countries, the majority of the citizens generally appreciate social ties and feelings of being socially accepted by others. As noted before, solidarity (Omobowale and Omobowale, 2019) and the urge to satisfy one's feeling for friendship, love and association, which are traditional values within Nigerian communities, could contribute to the choice of engaging in coworking spaces. Given that there are limited spaces for social interactions in the country, such as libraries or recreational parks, people welcome alternative spaces of social engagements in urban centres as opportunities to interact with peers with shared interests. Coworking spaces provide an opportunity to satisfy this yearning for social interaction and collaboration, as well as co-localisation among people from diverse fields of study or lines of trade (Spinuzzi, 2012).

The world, generally, is experiencing global warming and shortage in some environmental resources which have negatively affected the environment with some places experiencing unusual flooding, drought, water and land shortage (Zietsman, 2019). These *environmental factors* have significantly brought about modification in the utilisation of environmental resources in today's modern world. In Nigeria also, there have been drastic changes in the mode of utilising land resources, especially in major urban cities (like Lagos, Port-Harcourt, Abuja, etc.) which engendered the creation of multi-purpose buildings or multi-use facilities such as coworking spaces. In particular, the possibility of coworking spaces to provide more stable electricity and internet connection creates a conducive and productive environment to do business from. Furthermore, it is not only the maximisation of environmental resources but also the possibility of ensuring judicious utilisation of the land resource amongst a broader range of user groups that makes coworking spaces important.

The digital creative economy is of interest to young Nigerians because of the limitless opportunities provided by internet technologies (Michael and Samson, 2014). Across the world, cultural, social, economic and financial components of human societies have been redesigned as a result of the advancement in modern technologies. *Technological factors* and changes have boosted economic growth, job opportunities, service delivery, social networking and innovation as well as efficiency in both developed and developing countries on varying scales (Kelly and Firestone, 2016). Evidence gathered from literature reveals that the proceeds from the adoption and utilisation of modern technologies are more noticeable in developed countries than developing ones (Kelly and Firestone, 2016). With the increasing diffusion of modern technologies, particularly computer systems and internet, across regions of the world, there has been a push towards the development of incubation hubs, tech hubs, innovation spaces as well as coworking. In particular, the costs of internet connectivity and restraints in power availability make the concept of shared coworking spaces attractive to small-business owners and individuals in Nigeria.

The operation and expansion of coworking spaces in Nigerian societies present challenges that require urgent policy attention so as to avoid undermining the purpose of establishing coworking spaces in Nigeria. As mentioned, challenges like poor infrastructure and low levels of technology are often hard to address by individual providers. In our survey, we asked: "What could be done to facilitate the growth/ development of coworking in Nigeria?" Some of the responses offered insights on the role of policy. In general, most respondents acknowledged a lack of public support for businesses but also a lack of investment in facilities that could support socio-economic activities. A respondent considers the role of the public sector to support infrastructural investment.

> solar power as a sustainable energy source could take off a reasonable percentage of the running costs. However, the capital requirements are huge. Access to cheap loans can help coworking organisations take off.
>
> (respondent, Port Harcourt)

Similarly, another respondent highlights that coworking spaces take on a lot of developmental objectives and could be supported more broadly:

Coworking is a significant economic intervention so it cannot be sustainable without recognition from the government and being deliberate in planning along with it and supporting its growth.

(respondent, Abuja)

Many point to the importance for the government of coordinating access to specific infrastructure like "provision of funding, fast internet, power" (respondent, Kwara) and "broadband access, hub/government collaborations" (respondent, Uyo). Others also consider the role that government could play in educating and giving access to coworking spaces to the broader public:

government (which the masses already blame for the economic crunch) should model various PPP to provide coworking spaces for the public. More libraries should even be created with access to steady power supply and internet, which would help introduce the public to the importance to their business/personal life.

(respondent, Delta State)

Others highlight that more opportunities could be created for "collaboration between hubs" (respondent, Port Harcourt and Lagos) and for "more International Partnerships" (respondent, Akure).

For all the respondents, the government could play a more prominent role in coordinating, networking and facilitating the activities of the sector. This would generate economic growth but, more broadly, it would give access to opportunities for individuals who can access the benefit of coworking spaces.

Conclusions

This chapter addressed issues and reflections on the expansion and role of coworking in the development of Nigeria's creative economy and its future development. It joins the call made by others for the need to "de-westernise" knowledge about the creative economy and creative work (Alacovska and Gill, 2019). In particular, we argue it is essential to consider both the entrepreneurial and developmental agenda within coworking. It is not merely another business sector that is expanding globally, but a platform enabling economic and societal changes that might have a broader impact.

In Nigeria, the creation of coworking places is increasingly expanding, especially in major urban cities like Lagos, Abuja and Port-Harcourt. Here business individuals, professionals and students are interested in informal learning settings and activities that enhance collaboration, social networking and community development. Coworking spaces are designed to suit the needs of different categories of users (academics, business individuals, students and professionals) and to facilitate the social learning process that will significantly result in creativity, efficiency, idea generation and social networking. This chapter also affirms how coworking is not entirely new in Nigerian society because some of the features of coworking spaces align with the values of indigenous people in the country. However, the sector needs to address the challenges of financial constraints, poor infrastructure and a low level of access to technology, which could hamper its development.

Notwithstanding the challenges facing the survival of coworking spaces in Nigeria, there is still some assurance these spaces will thrive. As demonstrated by the data, there is an increasing trend in Nigeria for the development of new coworking spaces, which suggests it is responding to real demand for these services. Need for coworking spaces in developing countries is driven by business development needs and entrepreneurs, and this is not currently supported explicitly by any policy intervention. At the moment, policy does not seem involved or interested in the development of coworking opportunities. Beyond the private sector, there is a need for third-sector/development organisations to be more involved to support the development agenda within coworking. There is also a need to develop a wider coworking ecosystem involving a range of stakeholders to develop coworking and its policy. This would ensure that coworking not only thrives but can also provide opportunity from a wider sector of the population and be accessible across socio-economic classes.

More policy support is definitely needed for the infrastructural challenges that the country faces. Even though coworking spaces tend to be privately owned, for more consistent growth, it would be necessary for public policy to become involved in more PPP to support the economic development function of coworking and a more coordinated infrastructure provision.

Therefore, as the Venia (2017) coworking report highlights, the ability of coworking spaces to collaborate and share knowledge for expansion and development of the sector will be critical for the future development of the sector.

These are very early observations, and we intend to build on this research with further interviews and so seek to contribute to the development of the sector. In particular, it seems essential to consider the motivation of entrepreneurs within coworking structures and their ability to contribute to other developmental agendas in Nigeria. Furthermore, it would be important to consider questions of access and opportunities and how they are open (or not) to the broader Nigerian population, especially in consideration of gender, ethnic or class differences. If coworking has the potential to have a broader impact on supporting new businesses and the emergence of new ideas, it will be essential to question how this empowers Nigerian society at large or only a few groups within it.

Notes

1 All the data analysis on co-worker data was completed on 21 July 2020.
2 Google Trends application is a tool for analysing search behaviour relative to a particular country. It does not provide absolute search counts, but the metrics is designed to rate search queries within an index ranging from 1 to 10 (Jun et al., 2018).
3 All coworking spaces included in the publication were contacted via email and when possible via social media. A reminder was sent but the timing of the survey (end of summer 2019) may have negatively affected the overall response rate.
4 These numbers do not acknowledge the impact that the Covid-19 pandemic might have on coworking spaces globally and in Africa specifically. Our research took place before the 2020 pandemic and we cannot forecast its impact on the sector.

References

Adebayo S. and Olonisakin T. (2018) Nigeria: social identities and the struggle for survival. *Nigerian Journal of Social Psychology* 1(1): 176–197.
Agiri B. (1983) The development of wage labour in agriculture in Southern Yorubaland 1900–1940. *Journal of the Historical Society of Nigeria* 12(1/2): 95–107.
Akanle O. and Omotayo A. (2020) Youth, unemployment and incubation hubs in Southwest Nigeria. *African Journal of Science, Technology, Innovation and Development* 12(2): 165–172.
Alacovska A. and Gill R. (2019) De-westernizing creative labour studies: the informality of creative work from an ex-centric perspective. *International Journal of Cultural Studies* 22(2): 195–212.
Bakare O.O. and Kolawole C.Y. (2019) Potentials of Adire workshop in wealth creation among the youths. *Tropical Built Environment Journal* 6(2): 87–95.
Barredo J.I. and Demicheli L. (2003) Urban sustainability in developing countries' megacities: modelling and predicting future urban growth in Lagos. *Cities* 20(5): 297–310.
Bates T.W. (2011) *Community and Collaboration: New Shared Workplaces for Evolving Work Practices.* Cambridge, MA: Massachusetts Institute of Technology.

Bilandzic M. and Foth M. (2013) Libraries as coworking spaces: understanding user motivations and perceived barriers to social learning. *Library Hi Tech* 31(2): 254–273.

Bouncken R.B., Laudien S.M., Fredrich V., et al. (2018) Coopetition in coworking-spaces: value creation and appropriation tensions in an entrepreneurial space. *Review of Managerial Science* 12(2): 385–410.

Clarysse B., Wright M. and Van Hove J. (2015) *A Look Inside Accelerators.* London: Nesta.

Comunian R. and England L. (2020). Creative and cultural work without filters: Covid-19 and exposed precarity in the creative economy. *Cultural Trends* 29(2): 112–128.

Comunian R. and Jacobi S. (2021) Growing collaborative creative learning spaces: the case of London School of Mosaic. In: Montanari F., Mattarelli E. and Scapolan A. (eds) *The Collaborative Turn. How Collaborative Spaces Foster Collaboration and Creativity.* London: Routledge, pp. 268–281.

Fadipẹ N., Okediji Q.O. and Okediji F.O. (1970) *Sociology of the Yoruba.* Ibadan: UP.

Friederici N. (2018) Hope and hype in Africa's digital economy: the rise of innovation hubs. *Digital Economies at Global Margins.* Boston: MIT Press.

Fuzi A. (2015) Co-working spaces for promoting entrepreneurship in sparse regions: the case of South Wales. *Regional Studies, Regional Science* 2(1): 462–469.

Gandini A., Bandinelli C. and Cossu A. (2017) Collaborating, competing, co-working, coalescing. *Artists, freelancers and social entrepreneurs as the 'new subjects' of the creative economy.* In Graham J. and Gandini A. (eds) Collaborative Production in the Creative Industries. London: Westminster Press, pp. 15–32.

Jun S.-P., Yoo H.S. and Choi S. (2018) Ten years of research change using Google Trends: from the perspective of big data utilizations and applications. *Technological Forecasting and Social Change* 130: 69–87.

Kelly T. and Firestone R. (2016) How Tech Hubs are Helping to Drive Economic Growth in Africa: Background Report for World Bank. World Development Report 2016. Washington, DC: World Bank.

Kojo I. and Nenonen S. (2016) Typologies for co-working spaces in Finland – what and how? *Facilities* 34(5/6): 302–313.

Lumley R.M. (2014) A coworking project in the campus library: supporting and modeling entrepreneurial activity in the academic library. *New Review of Academic Librarianship* 20(1): 49–65.

Luo Y. and Chan R.C. (2020) Production of coworking spaces: evidence from Shenzhen, China. *Geoforum* 110: 97–105.

Mbakwe P.U. (2015) The impact of colonial rule on the agricultural economy of Mbaise, Imo State, 1500–1960. *African Journal of History and Culture* 7(6): 133–140.

McLaughlin P. and Faulkner J. (2012) Flexible spaces ... what students expect from university facilities. *Journal of Facilities Management* 110: 97–105.

Michael O.I. and Samson A.J. (2014) The impact of information and communication technology on youth and its vocational opportunities in Nigeria. *Journal of Good Governance and Sustainable Development in Africa* 2(1): 106–112.

Moriset B. (2013) *Building New Places of the Creative Economy. The Rise of Coworking Spaces.* Available at: https://halshs.archives-ouvertes.fr/halshs-00914075/document (accessed 21/07/2020).

Okpara J.O. and Kabongo J.D. (2009) An empirical evaluation of barriers hindering the growth of small and medium sized enterprises (SMEs) in a developing economy. *African Journal of Business and Economic Research* 4(1): 7–21.

Oldenburg R. (1989) *The Great Good Place: Cafés, Coffee Shops, Community Centers, Beauty Parlors, General Stores, Bars, Hangouts, and how they get you Through the Day.* Minnesota, MN: Paragon House Publishers.

Omobowale M.O. and Omobowale A.O. (2019) Oju and Inu: solidarity in the informal market space in Ibadan, Nigeria. *Journal of Black Studies* 50(4): 401–420.

Sargent K. and Daniels L. (2016) *Coworking: A Corporate Real Estate Perspective* Available at: https://workplaceinsight.net/wp-content/uploads/2016/10/HOK-Coworking-Report-A-CRE-Perspective-UK.pdf (accessed 13/08/2020).

Schmidt S., Brinks V. and Brinkhoff S. (2014) Innovation and creativity labs in Berlin: organizing temporary spatial configurations for innovations. *Zeitschrift für Wirtschaftsgeographie* 58(1): 232–247.

Spinuzzi C. (2012) Working alone together: coworking as emergent collaborative activity. *Journal of Business and Technical Communication* 26(4): 399–441.

UNCTAD (2018) *Creative Economy Outlook Trends in International Trade in Creative Industries Country Profiles.* Available at: https://unctad.org/en/PublicationsLibrary/ditcted2018d3_en.pdf.

Venia (2017) *Nigeria's First Coworking Report.* Available at: https://veniabusinesshub.com/nigeria-coworking-report/ (accessed 21/07/2020).

Wanyama F.O. (2009) *Cooperatives for African Development: Lessons From Experience. School of Development and Strategic Studies, Maseno University.* Maseno, Kenya: Maseno University.

Weijs-Perrée M., van de Koevering J., Appel-Meulenbroek R., et al. (2019) Analysing user preferences for co-working space characteristics. *Building Research and Information* 47(5): 534–548.

Yakubu O.M. (2002) Arts, crafts and indigenous industries in Nigeria. *Journal of Cultural Studies* 4(1): 215.

Zietsman J. (2019) *Framework for Developing Coworking Spaces Through Sustainable Refurbishment in South Africa.* Available at: https://scholar.sun.ac.za/bitstream/handle/10019.1/107276/zietsman_framework_2019.pdf?sequence=1 (accessed 20/08/2020).

Part II

Coworking

Policy and development

6 Coworking, gender and development
The case of Tribe XX Lab

Lauren England, Emalohi Iruobe and Roberta Comunian

Introduction

The academic literature on and policy interest towards coworking have been growing in the last decade. Although coworking is a global model for supporting entrepreneurship and is growing in many African countries, the chapter argues for the need to contextualise its development and understand issues of gender and access. In Nigeria, there are high levels of entrepreneurship and coworking is widely spread, yet women do not benefit from equality at the political level, which impacts their entrepreneurial activity; there is limited access to funding, a lack of mentors to provide guidance and stereotypes that block women from being accepted as experts and supervisors. Social norms continue to support male dominance in economic affairs, which can discourage self-confidence in female entrepreneurs.

In 2019 we conducted fieldwork in Lagos as part of an Arts and Humanities Research Council (AHRC) funded international research network[1], including interviews with seven representatives/owners of coworking spaces in the city reflecting on the challenges of entrepreneurship and how coworking responds to the needs of the creative entrepreneur. Within this broader context, we conducted an in-depth case study on the work of Tribe XX Lab, the only space we found that specifically targeted women. This case study involved studying the organisation's documents, reports and social media, as well as an interview with the director and a short observation of activities within the coworking space itself conducted by two of the authors (England and Comunian) during an afternoon.

Using the case study of Tribe XX Lab, the chapter addresses the gap in understanding of gender-based experiences of coworking. Through the case we can observe not only the ways in which the coworking space seeks to address the challenges facing female entrepreneurs in Nigeria,

DOI: 10.4324/9781003191681-6

but also the multifunctionality of the space and how it supports entrepreneurial and personal development on individual and collective levels, as well as acting as a space for activism and advocacy.

From here we position coworking spaces and collectives as multifunctional spaces. We argue that such organisations and business models that explicitly and specifically address and accommodate the needs of women have significant potential to act as a developmental tool to support gender equality and women's economic empowerment in developing economies.

Female entrepreneurship in Africa: value, social barriers and policy

In recent decades there has been a growing acknowledgement of the contribution of female entrepreneurs to economic development, particularly in developing economies (Adom, 2015; Mordi et al., 2010). This in part due to their high numbers – sub-Saharan Africa has the highest rate of female entrepreneurship globally (Olarewaju, 2019b). The encouragement of female-led micro-entrepreneurship in African countries is often positioned as a poverty alleviation measure, and solution to unemployment and gender-based occupational segregation (Mordi et al., 2010). Research also indicates that increasing female employment and empowerment can boost productivity and economic growth (Olarewaju, 2019a) and improve women's overall quality of life (Klasen and Lamanna, 2009).

It is however noted that attention paid to women's entrepreneurship in the African context has been limited in part due to their prominent operation in informal economies (Adom, 2015) and at subsistence level, with limited employees, revenues, profits and productivity (Diop, 2017: para. 2). Scarce employment opportunities and competition with men within the labour market are also seen as drivers for women in Nigeria to own their businesses (Mordi and Mmieh, 2009). However, efforts to promote women entrepreneurs must be broad-based and inclusive of their contributions across both formal and informal aspects of the economy.

The literature acknowledges a wide range of social, political and infrastructure-related challenges for entrepreneurs of all genders across Africa and in other developing economies, including policy, access to space, education and finance, among others (Igwe et al., 2018). While gender-based differences in access to start-up capital and various types of venture financing are acknowledged globally (Robichaud et al., 2019), this may be exacerbated in the African context by cultural values, gender stereotypes, limited collateral or a lack of important family ties, and higher rates of women establishing businesses in non-traditional industries and producing in informal and domestic contexts (Derera et al., 2014; Mordi et al., 2010). However, charitable and non-profit organisations actively engaging women may provide an alternative source of finance for women entrepreneurs, helping to address unequal access to bank credit (Grant, 2013).

Across sub-Saharan Africa, policy can play a vital role in both causing and addressing the challenges and barriers for female entrepreneurs (Moses and Mordi, 2010). In particular, there are calls for policies to promote gender parity in business and through education (Adom, 2015; Olarewaju, 2019a) but also to eliminate the negative impact of stereotypes and cultural traditions on female-owned businesses (Anambane and Adom, 2018) and enhance access to funding and business support for women entrepreneurs (Derera et al., 2014; Moses and Mordi, 2010).

Local and national economic, cultural and religious environments can underpin or exacerbate the challenges faced by entrepreneurs (Mordi et al., 2010; Kitching and Woldie, 2004). We address the specifics of our case context, Nigeria, later in the chapter before exploring how female-orientated coworking intersects with this environment as a facilitator of female entrepreneurship through the case study of Tribe XX Lab.

Coworking: growth, flexibility and inclusivity?

The academic literature on and policy interest towards coworking have been growing in the last decade. Coworking, simply put, is a shared working environment where people from different walks of life do their business. Coworking is a global model and is growing in many African countries, as discussed in Chapter 3, including Nigeria (BBC, 2019). Research has identified the role of coworking as a meaningful response to the high rate of unemployment in Nigeria, especially amongst youth (Akanle and Omotayo, 2020). However, to date, there is no acknowledgement of the potential role that coworking could play in addressing gender inequalities.

The literature on coworking has highlighted the role of such spaces in network formation and in supporting entrepreneurial development (Gandini, 2015). Weijs-Perrée et al.'s (2019) review of coworking literature highlighted how coworking spaces present an image of flexibility, accessibility and inclusivity. However, there is no specific study that highlights gendered dynamics or the gender (or diversity) of these spaces. Deskmag (2018) offers some general (global) statistics on the gender of users, with female participation increasing from 36.4% in 2016 to 40.7%

in 2018. They highlight that 26% of coworking spaces allow children but only 2% offer childcare. Cnossen and Knappert (2019) also identify that, in the Netherlands, despite a discourse of openness and professional diversity, existing societal inequalities are reproduced. There is further critique of the supposed "flexibility" of coworking spaces in relation to work–life balance (Orel, 2019) and as "family-friendly" (Lewis and Beauregard, 2018) spaces and how this relates to women. However, to date there has been a lack of attention given to how gender might influence coworking spaces or user experiences. For example, despite a growing trend in women co-workers, their numbers are very low for the age group that has childcare responsibilities (30–50) (Foertsch, 2017). Our understanding of female-only coworking spaces (Fletcher and Greenberg, 2018) is also limited. In this chapter we argue that such spaces may serve as an alternative model or demonstrate certain characteristics not found in mixed-gender or male-dominated spaces.

Furthermore, the focus on the Global North in coworking literature fails to take into account the specificities (social, economic, political and spatial) that impact the development of coworking spaces (and therefore entrepreneurship: De Bruin et al., 2007) in different contexts. It also creates a gap in our understanding of the different and multiple roles that different models of coworking spaces may play in developing economies, particularly in the context of women's role in economic development.

In this chapter we argue for the need to contextualise the development of coworking and understand issues of gender and access, particularly in the context of developing economies where specific cultural and socio-economic conditions may exacerbate known barriers to female entrepreneurship (Lewis, 2006), or create new obstacles and opportunities. In the next section, we outline the gender-specific challenges and policy barriers facing female entrepreneurs in Nigeria with a focus on access to space but also wider issues around gender equality.

Nigeria: gender-specific challenges and policy barriers for female entrepreneurs

Article 26 of the International Covenant on Civil and Political Rights (ICCPR) provides that all persons are equal before the law and are entitled without any discrimination to equal protection of the law. However, Mordi et al. (2010: 9) state that "often women in Nigeria are treated as minors and as subservient, even though the Nigerian constitution gives women equal rights as men". Gender inequality, therefore, remains a prevalent challenge in Nigeria, particularly concerning employment and entrepreneurship (ibid.).

For a long time, corporate jobs and businesses have been seen as "male-only" activities while women are designated as "wife" and "mother", tasked with caring responsibilities, domestic work or, at most, menial jobs (Zakaria, 2001). Woldie and Adersua (2004: 78) state: "the greatest challenge for Nigerian women in business is being taken seriously by their male counterparts, as well as in society as a whole". Nigerian women's entrepreneurial aspirations and activities are hence positioned in conflict with gender norms (Mordi et al., 2010), often associated with conservative values (Madichie, 2009) and religious philosophies (Mordi et al., 2010). While experienced by women in patriarchal societies (ibid.) within and beyond the African continent, in Nigeria there is a notably large power discrepancy which also creates expectations for men to be "the economic provider, emotional protector and leader" (Mordi et al., 2010: 9). These conservative socio-cultural values (and associated socio-inhibitions) are in turn embedded into policy, legal structures and institutional support mechanisms (Madichie, 2009; Mordi et al., 2010). Although policy initiatives have been associated with an increase in women pursuing higher education, career development and governance and executive positions, conflicts between work and family responsibilities remain (Eze, 2017).

Nigeria is reported to have the highest number of female entrepreneurs in the whole of Africa (BBC, 2017). To support greater (formal) market access and growth and reduce over-reliance on informal markets and/or domestic contexts (Mordi et al, 2010), there is a need for professional infrastructure (i.e. office space, internet, etc.). While infrastructure is needed by entrepreneurs of all genders, Nigeria's male dominance is reflected in land ownership (Ajala, 2017), meaning women often have to deal with male landlords. The perceptions of (working) women described above then create particular challenges in renting office space and other forms of accommodation, especially as independent tenants – a man must vouch that a woman is "decent" and can afford the rent, reflecting "a remnant of the idea that a woman has to be married or under her parents to be seen as decent" (Salaudeen, 2019: para. 9). Even after space is acquired, there is the fear of sexual harassment and violence (Johnson, 2010).

While a Gender Equality Bill was first introduced in March 2016, it was immediately shut down by the Nigerian Senate. Senators argued that the constitution already contained laws against the discrimination of all persons in Nigeria and that the bill was against both the Bible and the history of Nigeria in general, as well as against the Sharia law of the northern states (Adebayo, 2016). In 2019, Bukola Saraki, the Senate President of Nigeria, re-introduced the re-worked Gender Equality Bill and it finally started to gain the approval of senators (Iroanusi, 2019). The bill seeks to guarantee:

> the rights of women to equal opportunities in employment; equal rights to inheritance for both male and female children; equal rights for women in marriage and divorce, and equal access to education, property/land ownership and inheritance. It also seeks to protect the rights of widows; guarantee appropriate measures against gender discrimination in political and public life and ensure the prohibition of violence towards women.
>
> (ibid., para 4)

This is indicative of positive change and a reduction in gender inequality in Nigeria, although women's subjugated role in society must continue to be challenged if the potential of women's entrepreneurship is to be realised. The issues highlighted in this section are just examples of the many challenges plaguing women that were considered by the founder of the Tribe XX Lab in opening the first and only female coworking space in Nigeria in 2018.

Tribe XX Lab

Tribe XX Lab opened its doors to women in a range of fields on 8 March 2018, International Women's Day, in order to serve as a safe, comfortable and affordable space where the needs of women matter and are also met. Located on Lagos Island, the space has attracted female entrepreneurs across categories from craft, hair care and lingerie to computer programming and consultancy. Businesses must have at least one female founder in order to rent a space and an informal screening is conducted for suitability – excluding activities such as gambling. By 2020, Tribe XX Lab had helped over 120 women to develop and scale up their businesses.

The goal of Tribe XX Lab was to further help women who are economically independent, providing them with a professional space so their individual businesses can be taken seriously while also providing a community of women that not only looks out for their business but also their wellbeing as a woman. Tribe XX Lab also helps with the advocacy of women's rights and the leaders are activists who help challenge and bring to light national issues involving women.

Tribe XX Lab is the first and only co-working and wellness space exclusively for women in Nigeria. We have evolved into a collective of women working together to get each other a seat at the table by creating a space that fosters community, balance and growth.

(Tribe XX Lab website)

In this mission, the multifunctionality of the organisation can be observed. In the following sections, we identify in greater detail the different strands of Tribe XX Lab and how these go beyond standard functions of coworking spaces (i.e. access to flexible space and networking) to address the political and social issues for women in Nigeria identified above.

Business development: access to space and professionalisation

Tribe XX Lab was founded partly in response to the challenge of access to space for female entrepreneurs. A key area of work for Tribe XX Lab is therefore in removing barriers to entrepreneurship and economic independence for women in Nigeria. Through the provision of physical infrastructure specifically for women (although not excluding men associated with female-owned businesses) they seek not only to address the challenges acknowledged above, but also propose models for change, particularly in relation to access to space. Tribe XX offers rental space on a membership basis for regular users, but also on a day rate to enable greater flexibility.

The founder of Tribe XX Lab highlighted how access to office (coworking) space provides more than physical infrastructure. It also comes with associated professional services and enables women to project a professional image which creates a "ripple" effect of economic independence and female empowerment:

the idea is to help women become economically independent [...] there's a ripple effect of economic independence, which is, you know, maybe a woman is in a bad situation, maybe she's remaining in her marriage because her husband is the sole bread winner [...] We provide you admin, you get your office, get your mail here, you can make your business cards, your letterhead with your own company name with the office address [...] so people's businesses are getting more professional, or they're getting a more professional front.

(Tribe XX Lab Founder)

She also noted that in Nigeria, appearances matter, and having office space and a professional front to one's business is key to addressing clients' perceptions of entrepreneurial ability:

> there's a thing in Nigeria that I notice is that a lot of people judge on appearance. And so you may be a stellar attorney right [...] if you have a client meeting in a cafe, most likely person is going to be like "nah, I don't think this person is capable", just because they don't see you in an office.
>
> (Tribe XX Lab Founder)

Education and training: upskilling and reskilling

A second area of work for Tribe XX Lab is in upskilling and reskilling women, with the aim of creating value for Nigerian society and the economy. Education and training programmes hosted and run by the space (sometimes for free) have focused on business skills and science, technology, engineering and mathematics (STEM) skills, including coding. For example, Tribe Tech is a programme aimed at reskilling and upskilling in STEM/coding, conducted in partnership with chemistry students from the University of Lagos and Kabara Community Initiative, a non-profit organisation encouraging and fostering STEM in girls from Northern Nigeria. Programmes such as this help to address barriers for women entering STEM education and careers by providing relevant education and training, but also role models of women in STEM.

> University of Lagos with their students came to us [...] because they're interested in STEM but a lot of women drop out because it's dominated by men [...] they asked us to sponsor them once a month to come into our space and have training on anything to do with STEM. [...] there's a huge concentration now of getting more and more women into STEM and they need to feel that there are other women like them.
>
> (Tribe XX Lab Founder)

Tribe XX Lab's Accelerator for women also equips participants with funding, training and access to an investor network, supporting economic growth which in turn has the capacity to lift people out of poverty. In 2019, Tribe XX Lab partnered with certified digital skills trainers from Google to offer free training in core digital skills to 320 women. They also hosted the She Leads Africa conference in 2018 and 2019.

Partnerships and external collaborations were important to achieve a wider reach, leverage support and funding and offer opportunities for members to interact with national and international organisations. The Founder saw the Lab as serving an intermediary function here in connecting members with larger, high-profile companies – such as Google or Facebook – through events and training activities, but also offering such companies access to talent and an audience of women entrepreneurs.

Community and wellness: accommodating the needs of women

The wellness aspect of Tribe XX Lab is one of its unique features. Both the business model and the physical space have been designed to include wellbeing support and provide services and space that promote self-care and address the specific needs of women (Fletcher and Greenberg, 2018). For example, sanitary products are provided, there is a designated nap room for members and the space is child-friendly. The overall aesthetic (layout, colour pallet, etc.) of the space (Figure 6.1) was consciously curated to create a calming environment.

> The fundamental idea is to create a place where women can come together, network, make friendships, have somewhere comfortable to work and just be themselves. [...] We believe strongly that with the responsibilities unfairly placed on women, it is imperative to make self-care a priority.
>
> (Tribe XX Lab website)

There is a regular social calendar, a bar and free wellbeing activities such as yoga. The space also supports non-member businesses (female-owned/orientated) including partnerships with local restaurants, stocking products and hosting pop-up events. The art on the walls (by female artists) is rotated regularly to give different artists exposure.

> the average Nigerian woman is expected to handle all domestic issues, all childcare, still run her business, and go to work and still look pretty, right. So it's a lot of work. But if you come into a space that emphasizes your wellness, so you can get organic skincare products, you can get organic snacks, we have community [...] And you can collaborate with other members of the tribe.
>
> (Tribe XX Lab Founder)

Community building is integral to the language and structure of Tribe XX Lab. The coming together of women and encouragement of

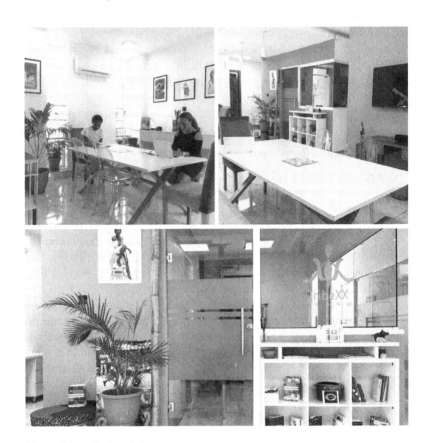

Figure 6.1 Tribe XX Lab space.
Source: Courtesy of Tribe XX.

collaboration between members were seen to be integral to fostering a sense of collective empowerment. This includes traditional aspects of coworking such as networking and collaboration (Weijs-Perrée et al., 2019). A willingness to support and collaborate with others in addition to pursuing independent work are also criteria the Tribe leaders look for when building their member base.

Advocacy

Another key strand of Tribe XX Lab is advocacy for women's rights. In this way Tribe XX Lab positions itself as an "umbrella" system to support women, especially young women, in challenging societal expectations and "prescriptions" for women's lives in Nigeria by providing a safe space for discussion, debate and activism.

> We had an event [in] partnership with an online community called The Girls Like Me. [...] We were talking about issues of identity, of being who you are in a society that really has a prescription for how your life should be. [...] "don't be too ambitious, get married, have kids, stay home, take care of your husband. Be obedient" [...] Nobody's having that conversation now with Generation Z. And even with some millennials because of this engrained idea. So this is why we are here.
>
> (Tribe XX Lab Founder)

Advocacy work has included encouraging and supporting the coordination and promotion (via social media) of larger campaigns and protests such as the Market March[2] against sexual harassment and bullying in marketplaces; the Market March was initiated at The Girls Like Me event when one of the young women stood up and said she was tired of being harassed when going to the market.

> we went on and marched, everybody walked through the market, we had signs that said "don't touch us". And were on the news and all of that stuff. And it's just really the time where women, young women are saying, enough is enough. And so they need that support, we want to be that umbrella that supports and helps them.
>
> (Tribe XX Lab Founder)

Events such as The Girls Like Me conversation and the Tribe XX virtual summer festival, XX-CEED 2020, provide opportunities for both local and international audiences to learn about and engage with social issues around gender and race (in)equality. In May 2020, Tribe XX Lab also received grant funding from Voice Global on behalf of the government of the Netherlands for their social justice and empowerment movement to end sex for grades in universities in Nigeria. The project "IGOTALK", a pidgin-language phrase meaning "I will not be silent", "I will tell on you", highlights the voices of young women facing exploitation and abuse in higher-education institutions in Nigeria as well as enlightening the public on the magnitude of the problem. Its purpose is to empower women and youths through empathy and strength in numbers to know and demand their rights. It serves as a warning to perpetrators that the silence of victims will no longer protect them as well as giving an avenue for victims to tell their stories of survival.

A model for female empowerment and economic development through coworking

From the case study presented here and illustrated in Figure 6.2, we can understand coworking spaces such as Tribe XX Lab as multifunctional models for supporting female empowerment and entrepreneurial development. We argue that this shows how the coworking model can go beyond infrastructure provision and be tailored to help to address the challenges faced by female entrepreneurs, in Nigeria and beyond. From this model we position coworking spaces and collectives as having the potential to act as a developmental tool to support gender equality and women's economic empowerment in developing economies.

It was noted that the emphasis on female wellbeing within the business model of Tribe XX Lab was not understood or welcomed by male investors when the founder was seeking initial funding: "when I was trying to start and I was looking for investors for the space they all happened to be men, and they all wanted to change the heart of what I wanted to do" (Founder). The space was subsequently secured via family connections; however, their continued presence and success were seen to provide a "proof of concept" for the business model and had attracted interest and support from national and international organisations looking to support hubs and entrepreneurship in Nigeria, including the Lagos State Employment Trust Fund[3] and the British Council Creative Enterprise Support Programme.[4] As the first of its kind in Nigeria, Tribe XX Lab has ambitions for expansion and potentially franchising across Nigeria and Africa.

In order to facilitate the empowerment of women that will positively contribute to both the economy and society in Nigeria and beyond, it is important that policy makers and business stakeholders recognise business models and spaces that address the specific experiences and needs of women entrepreneurs, and support their long-term sustainability and growth.

Conclusion

This chapter has sought to address the gap in our understanding of the different and multiple roles that different models of coworking spaces may play in developing economies, particularly in the context of women's role in economic development. By focusing on the

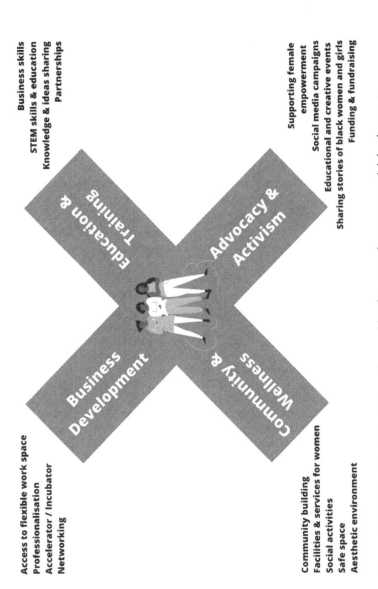

Business skills
STEM skills & education
Knowledge & ideas sharing
Partnerships

Supporting female empowerment
Social media campaigns
Educational and creative events
Sharing stories of black women and girls
Funding & fundraising

Education & Training

Advocacy & Activism

Business Development

Community & Wellness

Access to flexible work space
Professionalisation
Accelerator / Incubator
Networking

Community building
Facilities & services for women
Social activities
Safe space
Aesthetic environment

Figure 6.2 Multifunctionality of (female) coworking for women's entrepreneurial development.
Note: STEM, science, technology, engineering and mathematics.

specific context of Nigeria, it aims to take into account the specificities (social, economic, political and spatial) that impact the development of coworking spaces and (women's) entrepreneurship (De Bruin et al., 2007) in this country but which may also be relevant to the experiences of women in other African and Global South contexts. In the words of Tribe XX Lab Founder:

> Women are now seen every day both on social platforms and in person, breaking barriers and challenging the double standards set in place by years of patriarchy. Women of Tribe XX Lab are also playing their own part in recognizing the ills women face in society and providing solutions, going as far as lending their voices to women who are afraid to challenge these issues or are not privileged enough to. Renting apartments and offices should not be connected to gender but to the readiness and ability to live in or use such spaces. Women have been policed and guided by archaic traditions and beliefs for years and coming together as a tribe and addressing these issues offers a method to drive change.
>
> (Tribe XX Lab Founder)

Notes

1 The AHRC funded international research network connected to the Global Challenges Research Fund (GCRF) was entitled "Understanding and Supporting Creative Economies in Africa: Education, Networks and Policy", grant number AH/P005950/1 (2016–2019).
2 A number of market marches took place Lagos in 2019 with the goal of ending the normalised sexual harassment and bullying of women in markets. There is an associated online petition to push for better law enforcement.
3 In 2019 Tribe XX Lab was recognised and supported by the Lagos State Employment Trust Fund through the LSETF Hub Voucher programme which pays up to 70% off the membership fees for women requiring space and opportunities within the start-up ecosystem.
4 Tribe XX Lab was selected for the 2019 programme to participate in capacity-building masterclasses to increase their effectiveness in supporting entrepreneurs in the creative industries.

References

Adebayo, T.-H. 2016. How Yerima, Aliero, others led Senate onslaught against Gender Equality Bill. *Premium Times Nigeria*, 16/03/2016.
Adom, K. 2015. Recognizing the contribution of female entrepreneurs in economic development in sub-Saharan Africa: some evidence from Ghana. *Journal of Developmental Entrepreneurship*, 20, 1550003.

Ajala, T. 2017. Gender discrimination in land ownership and the alleviation of women's poverty in Nigeria: a call for new equities. *International Journal of Discrimination and the Law*, 17, 51–66.

Akanle, O. & Omotayo, A. 2020. Youth, unemployment and incubation hubs in Southwest Nigeria. *African Journal of Science, Technology, Innovation and Development*, 12, 165–172.

Anambane, G. & Adom, K. 2018. Assessing the role of culture in female entrepreneurship in contemporary sub-Saharan society: insights from the Nabadam district of Ghana. *Journal of Developmental Entrepreneurship*, 23, 1850017.

BBC. 2017. *The businesswomen in Nigeria making money out of moi moi.* Available: www.bbc.co.uk/news/av/world-africa-38918048 (accessed 18/08/2020).

BBC. 2019. *The rise of co-working in Nigeria.* Available: www.bbc.co.uk/news/av/business-48889007 (accessed 19/08/2020).

Cnossen, B. & Knappert, L. 2019. Inclusion in coworking spaces: tension and struggle in an emerging field. Academy of Management Proceedings. Briarcliff Manor, NY: Academy of Management, p. 15500.

De Bruin, A., Brush, C. G. & Welter, F. 2007. Advancing a framework for coherent research on women's entrepreneurship. *Entrepreneurship Theory and Practice*, 31, 323–339.

Derera, E., Chitakunye, P. & O'Neill, C. 2014. The impact of gender on start-up capital: a case of women entrepreneurs in South Africa. *The Journal of Entrepreneurship*, 23, 95–114.

Deskmag. 2018. *The 2018 state of coworking.* Available: www.deskmag.com/en/the-state-of-coworking-spaces-in-2018-market-research-development-survey/2 (accessed 18/08/2020).

Diop, M. 2017. Unleashing the potential of women entrepreneurs in Africa. Available: https://blogs.worldbank.org/nasikiliza/unleashing-the-potential-of-women-entrepreneurs-in-africa (accessed 08/04/2017).

Eze, N. 2017. *Balancing Career and Family: The Nigerian Woman's Experience.* PhD, Walden University.

Fletcher, K. A. & Greenberg, A. 2018. WSC Podcast Episode 4: Designing Coworking Spaces for Women. *The Work Science Centre Podcast.*

Foertsch, C. 2017. *The members: who works in coworking spaces?* Available: www.deskmag.com/en/members-of-coworking-spaces-demographics-statistics-global-survey-coworkers-research-2017 (accessed 18/08/2020).

Gandini, A. 2015. The rise of coworking spaces: a literature review. *ephemera*, 15, 193.

Grant, R. 2013. Gendered spaces of informal entrepreneurship in Soweto, South Africa. *Urban Geography*, 34, 86–108.

Igwe, P. A., Onjewu, A. E. & Nwibo, S. U. 2018. Entrepreneurship and SMEs' productivity challenges in sub-Saharan Africa. In: Dana, L.-P., Ratten, V. & Honyenuga, B. Q. (eds.) *African Entrepreneurship.* Cham, Switzerland: Palgrave MacMillan, pp. 189–221.

Iroanusi, Q. E. 2019. Senator reintroduces Gender Equality Bill. *Premium Times Nigeria*, 26/11/2019.

Johnson, K. 2010. Sexual harassment in the workplace: a case study of Nigeria. *Gender and Behaviour*, 8, 2903–2918.

Kitching, B. & Woldie, A. 2004. Female entrepreneurs in transitional economies: a comparative study of businesswomen in Nigeria and China. Conference Proceedings, 4th Annual Hawaii International Conference on Business, pp. 1–19.

Klasen, S. & Lamanna, F. 2009. The impact of gender inequality in education and employment on economic growth: new evidence for a panel of countries. *Feminist Economics*, 15, 91–132.

Lewis, P. 2006. The quest for invisibility: female entrepreneurs and the masculine norm of entrepreneurship. *Gender, Work and Organization*, 13(5), 453–469.

Lewis, S. & Beauregard, T. A. 2018. The meanings of work–life balance: a cultural perspective. In: Shockley, K., Shen, W. & Johnson, R. (eds.) *The Cambridge Handbook of the Global Work–Family Interface.* Cambridge, UK: Cambridge University Press, pp. 720–732.

Madichie, N. O. 2009. Breaking the glass ceiling in Nigeria: a review of women's entrepreneurship. *Journal of African Business*, 10, 51–66.

Mordi, C. & Mmieh, F. 2009. Divided labour and divided in-firm markets in the Nigerian petroleum sector. Proceedings of the 10th International Academy of African Business and Development Conference, 2009, pp. 19–23.

Mordi, C., Simpson, R., Singh, S. & Okafor, C. 2010. The role of cultural values in understanding the challenges faced by female entrepreneurs in Nigeria. *Gender in Management: An International Journal*, 25(1), 5–21.

Moses, C. & Mordi, C. 2010. Women entrepreneurship development in Nigeria: the effect of environmental factors. *Buletinul Universitatii Petrol-Gaze din Ploie~ ti*, 62, 43–52.

Olarewaju, T. I. 2019a. Can equalizing educational endowments between men and women create more female self-employed value in Nigeria? *Journal of Creating Value*, 5, 68–83.

Olarewaju, T. I. 2019b. Nigerian women entrepreneurs draw the short straw on education levels. Available: https://theconversation.com/nigerian-women-entrepreneurs-draw-the-short-straw-on-education-levels-112843 (accessed 18/08/2020).

Orel, M. 2019. Supporting work–life balance with the use of coworking spaces. *Equality, Diversity and Inclusion: An International Journal*, 39(5), 549–565.

Robichaud, Y., Cachon, J.-C. & McGraw, E. 2019. Gender differences in venture financing: a study among Canadian and US entrepreneurs. *Journal of Developmental Entrepreneurship*, 24, 1950014.

Salaudeen, A. 2019. Single women cannot rent property in Nigeria. Available: www.stearsng.com/article/single-women-cannot-rent-property-in-nigeria (accessed 01/02/2019).

Weijs-Perrée, M., Van De Koevering, J., Appel-Meulenbroek, R. & Arentze, T. 2019. Analysing user preferences for co-working space characteristics. *Building Research and Information*, 47, 534–548.

Woldie, A. & Adersua, A. 2004. Female entrepreneurs in a transitional economy. *International Journal of Social Economics*, 31(1/2), 78–93.

Zakaria, Y. 2001. Entrepreneurs at home: secluded Muslim women and hidden economic activities in Northern Nigeria. *Nordic Journal of African Studies*, 10, 107–123.

7 Ahead of policy? Creative hubs in East African cities

Ayeta Anne Wangusa, Roberta Comunian and Brian J. Hracs

Introduction

A wide and diverse body of literature has emerged around the theme of coworking (Gandini, 2015). Most literature considers the role played by the knowledge economy and new modes of post-industrial production and work. On one hand, the changes in the economy were leaving many large industrial buildings available to be regenerated in urban areas (Chatterton, 2000). On the other hand, a new class of creative, independent, freelance workers was emerging to reuse these spaces with new models of work (Florida, 2002). Both developments occurred as the creative and cultural industries (CCIs) emerged as a potential new tool for urban, local and regional development (Comunian et al., 2010).

Therefore, cities represent the ideal backdrop for the development of coworking initiatives. This development has gone hand in hand with the rise of new modes of production within the knowledge and creative economy, such as 'start-ups', 'social innovation' and the 'sharing economy' (Botsman and Rogers, 2011). Moriset (2013) describes coworking spaces in cities as 'third places', highlighting their hybrid nature somewhere in between home and work. Spinuzzi (2012) argues that coworking spaces are not just flexible shared office spaces for creative professionals 'working alone together', but a new form of urban social infrastructure enabling contacts and collaborations between people, ideas and connecting places (Merkel, 2015). Furthermore, the coworking concept can be conceived as a 'movement' or a 'philosophy' characterised by four common values – collaboration, openness, community and sustainability (Reed, 2007) – and may not necessarily be business-oriented, but aim at building a network of social relations within members of the coworking space. Also Leforestier (2009) attests to the view that the coworking practice is an 'open source community approach' to work that seeks to establish communitarian social

DOI: 10.4324/9781003191681-7

relations among the member-workers. Further research by Capdevila (2013) conceives coworking spaces as 'microclusters' that enable knowledge transfer among members from a network-based perspective.

As highlighted in Chapter 2, there is a wider range of literature and research on coworking spaces in the Global North (Waters-Lynch et al., 2016) and booming cities within East Asia (Luo and Chan, 2020), yet there is very little acknowledgement of the way the phenomenon has spread across the Global South (Shiach et al., 2017; Tintiangko and Soriano, 2020) and Africa in particular. This chapter addresses this gap by studying the emergence of hubs and coworking spaces in East Africa. Firstly, we will provide an overview on the emergence of coworking in East Africa and the differences between coworking spaces and creative hubs. We will then present the current knowledge and literature on creative hubs internationally. Secondly, we will focus on three creative hubs in three East African cities: the GoDown Arts Centre in Nairobi (Kenya), the Culture and Development East Africa (CDEA) hub in Dar es Salaam (Tanzania) and the Design Hub in Kampala (Uganda). For each case study the chapter explores their history and establishment, their location within their specific city and the kinds of CCIs and creative workers they host and support. In the third part of the chapter we specifically reflect on the relationship between the development of these creative hubs and policy. Here we consider both national-level industrial and cultural policy in the three countries (Kenya, Tanzania and Uganda) and urban development and cultural policy in the context of the three cities. Finally, we conclude by considering the challenges and opportunities that the development of these three hubs offer in the context of East Africa. In so doing, we also reflect on how Covid-19 might disrupt the coworking model and undermine exchanges and collaboration across CCIs and creative workers.

It is important to highlight that these reflections are based on ongoing doctoral research based at the University of Leicester (UK), that more broadly explores the connections of creative entrepreneurs in the East African creative hubs with questions of sustainable consumption and production.

From coworking to creative hubs: literature and developments

Emerging coworking dynamics in East Africa

As reported in Chapter 3, in the last five years there has been a sharp rise in the number of coworking spaces in Africa. However, the coworking space concept – especially in Africa, where the knowledge and opportunities offered by the creative economy are not so widely spread – remains mostly associated with the technological and digital sector and its companies. While the actors might not be the same, the coworking phenomenon is interesting because it is connected with broader developments and needs within the African economy and its workers and specifically its youth. Figure 7.1 highlights the quick spread of coworking spaces across East Africa, with some cities clearly concentrating a high number of coworking hubs, specifically Nairobi with thirty-nine hubs, Kampala with eight and Dar es Salaam with two. However, the map is not inclusive of creative hubs that also have coworking spaces.

While the phenomenon of coworking is ever expanding and involves companies more broadly in the knowledge and technological sectors, the concept of creative hubs connects more closely with work related to the emergence of the creative economy (UNDP and UNESCO, 2013) and the renewed importance of the CCIs as a sector. The CCIs have been defined in many different ways but it is widely acknowledged that they are industries and workers concerned with the production and provision of cultural and creative products – goods, services and experiences that are appreciated and valued for their aesthetic, communication or cultural component rather than their utilitarian function. In emerging economies like the ones of East Africa the creative economy is looked at as a potential sector for future development (British Council, 2013) but has not yet acquired the international profile it has in other African countries, as in the case of Nigeria and Nollywood. However, we argue that the combination of the rise of coworking as a development model and the creative economy could create further opportunities for development.

From coworking to creative hubs

In fact, for certain aspects the concept of creative hub represents a mix of both the creative clusters dynamics, common in fully developed creative economies, and the hub/coworking ideas (Figure 7.2). In relation to the former, they are CCI-specific and contribute to place-based regeneration and developing a shared knowledge pool (Chapain and Comunian, 2010). In connection with the latter they offer opportunities for start-ups and shared resources as well as collaborative working and training.

The concept of hubs has been broadly used in communication network design since the 1990s (Lee et al., 1993) and later within urban studies (Rantisi, 2002) and media studies (Hayden and Ball-Rokeach, 2007) to denote meeting points for materials, information and people

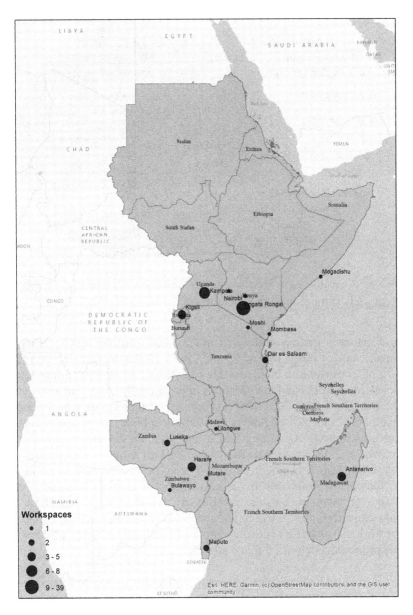

Figure 7.1 East African countries and coworking spaces.
Source: Data from Co-worker.com, accessed 23 July 2020.

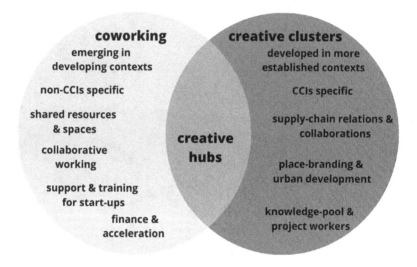

Figure 7.2 Creative hubs: bringing together coworking and creative clustering.
Note: CCIs, cultural and creative industries.

in a network, densely connected nodes where physical and informational changes occur (Shiach et al., 2017). In the creative sector, the idea of a creative hub builds on this knowledge and has been applied in policy frameworks and interventions internationally and particularly in the UK. Here, since 2003 there has been great emphasis on considering creative hubs as part of regional development policy as initiatives that nurture connections and exchange and vital for boosting economic activity and urban regeneration (ibid.). With a more international focus, the British Council (2015) has been an international promoter of the creative hub concept, as an idea that is commonly associated with other terms such as the 'creative city' and the 'creative economy'. Consequently, hubs have been understood as places that provide a space for work, participation and consumption. The British Council (2015: 4) has proposed a definition that states that:

> A creative hub is a place, either physical or virtual, which brings creative people together. It is a convenor, providing space and support for networking, business development and community engagement within the creative, cultural and tech sectors.

As a result, creative hubs are fast becoming a worldwide phenomenon. Most cities in the UK now host a thriving number of creative hubs.

Dovey et al. (2016) state that hubs have become a new way of organising creative economy innovation and development. The management and operation of a hub are primarily about the careful selection and compatibility of tenants and the 'animation' of the interaction between the actors and activities based on a clear understanding of the values of the hub (ibid.). According to the British Council, creative hubs tend to mean many things; however, it is difficult to prescribe a one-size-fits-all definition. Nevertheless, it is important to note that diversity is embedded in the DNA of creative hubs and each of them has different characteristics (British Council, 2015).

Furthermore, Sedini et al. (2014) have identified six components involved in the creation of creative hubs. These are incubators, specialist cultural service providers for companies and artists, virtual platforms, development agencies, coworking facilities and clusters. These components therefore broaden the parameters of a creative hub and validate the description of the hub as a node with a concentration of services, information and social relationships. In fact, Dovey et al. (2016) suggest that the diversity of hubs enables practitioners to fit their creative activity to a specific context. They, however, note that creative hubs are associated with other types of industrial agglomeration such as the cluster concept. The difference, however, is that while creative clustering within the creative economy is aligned with 'creative city' policy and industrial policy theory of the physical environment of cities and the cultural milieu, creative hubs tend to be localised in an urban cultural system of consumption and production.

Creative hubs in three East African cities: Nairobi, Dar es Salaam and Kampala

In order to explore in more detail the importance of creative hubs in the development of CCIs in East Africa, we focus on the creative hubs of three East African cities as a case study and consider their distinct structure and history, with specific emphasis on their urban location – and engagement with urban regeneration – as well as their users and creative communities that operate from those hubs.

GoDown Arts Centre (Nairobi, Kenya)

GoDown Arts Centre in Nairobi is the hub for Kenyan creativity in arts and media (Figure 7.3). Established in 2003, in a space that was formerly a car repair warehouse, the centre has contributed significantly to the growth, recognition and visibility of local artists.

Figure 7.3 GoDown Arts Centre.
Source: Courtesy of GoDown Arts Centre.

GoDown resonates with Capdevila's theory (2013) of coworking enabling knowledge transfer among hub members. This can be illustrated by the way the centre fosters and facilitates collaborations and encounters between artists from different disciplines and different parts of the world (GoDown Arts Centre, 2020).

GoDown Arts Centre is located in an industrial area, which has involved purchasing or leasing old and disused industrial buildings. In this case the location of the hub was not guided by policy, but by the availability of suitable space. Joy Mboya, founder of the GoDown Arts Centre, stated in an interview that:

> Locating the GoDown in the industrial area wasn't a deliberate choice but rather the result of not finding space in initially preferred areas; areas we thought would be closer to target audiences at the time. However, the industrial area location, being close to the larger population of the city (lower middle-income groups) has actually been a boon. Because of our location, we have learned to

have a more holistic perception of city and audiences, and been more reflective about the role of our organisation in national, city/community life and affairs.

The GoDown's resident clients in Nairobi are in the field of digital creativity, music recording and archiving, graphic design and advertising, festival organising, TV and music production, contemporary dance and filming of music videos. For the GoDown emphasis is placed on promoting the intrinsic value of culture – the imperative of freedom of artistic expression – and not aiming at value addition of Kenya's productive sectors.

Design Hub (Kampala, Uganda)

Design Hub Kampala (DHK), which was founded in 2017, is Uganda's first design coworking space located in Kampala's industrial area (Figure 7.4). The packages for the coworking space and service are for

Figure 7.4 Design Hub Kampala spaces.
Source: Courtesy of Design Hub Kampala.

three categories of clients: start-up, expanding and established. The hub has a mix of Ugandan and expat companies in design, media and policy space.

According to creative director Jantien Zuurbier, DHK aims to broaden the understanding of the field of design. Rusk (2011) points out the role of design in change management in the creative city hub to achieve economic development and urban regeneration based on the premise that traditional business models no longer fit our time.

As Zuurbier (in De Jong, 2017, para. 6) says:

> The idea is to broaden the field of design. In Uganda many people still think of design as decoration: making things pretty. But design is connected to many fields like communication and education. We try to stimulate co-creation and promote design-thinking as a whole.

Furthermore, a new dimension that DHK adds to the concept of coworking is co-creation (De Jong, 2017). The idea is to encourage a collaborative work environment where different people (entrepreneurs, freelancers, designers, writers, product developers, marketing minds, tech start-ups and makers) are able to co-design and co-create innovative solutions. The DHK approach combines the idea of coworking – social relations, ideas and workspace and coworking – with working collaboratively on a task or assignment.

In reference to its location, in an industrial area, according to Jean Kukunda, the Community Director of DHK, the choice to locate the hub in an industrial area was because the noise standards and control regulations (2003) for the Kampala City Council Authority (KCCA) are more flexible in industrial areas, with 70 db (day) and 60 db (night), which is suitable for activities like events (KCCA, 2003).

Culture and Development East Africa (CDEA) (Dar es Salaam, Tanzania)

CDEA was established in 2011 and is a creative think tank based in Dar es Salaam, whose core business is not providing coworking services: it has transformed a section of its office into a coworking space. 'Hot seaters' is CDEA's coinage for hot desking where start-ups or solo representatives from media firms hire a seat round a shared long desk. CDEA is located in a mixed-use residential area, a location that was informed by the decision to be in a middle-income area that was also close to institutions of learning. CDEA also hosts a creative

Figure 7.5 Culture and Development East Africa (CDEA) spaces.
Source: Courtesy of CDEA.

economy incubator, an arts space (Eco Sanaa Terrace) for events, with a lounge area where the 'hot seaters' can meet their guests and capacity-building programmes for artists and creative entrepreneurs (see Figure 7.5). This structure resonates with the perspective of Sedini et al. (2014) on the key components of a creative hub. CDEA 'hotseaters' include start-ups in communications, creative makers, CCI policy advocacy and non-governmental organisations (NGOs) in the social sector. The hub also has a creative economy incubator and accelerator initiative that offers technical and business skills to fashion and accessories designers, interior and exterior designers, filmmakers and musicians.

Policy agendas and coworking hubs in East Africa

Building on the case studies, we argue that is important to consider how their work might connect and empower (or be empowered by) broader policy actions and interventions. Here it is important to connect three areas of policy: the overall national industrial policies of the countries, the urban development policies of the cities and finally the national cultural policy.

National industrial policy and 'creativity'

The national industrialisation and strategies for Kenya (Kenya Ministry of Industralization, 2012), Uganda (Uganda Ministry Of Trade, Industry & Cooperatives, 2020) and Tanzania (Tanzania Ministry of Trade and Industry, 1996) have prioritised sub-sectors that require value addition which include some sectors in which creative entrepreneurs can add to the value chains. These include textiles and clothing, leather products leather, glass products and recycling materials for Kenya and Tanzania and cosmetics for Uganda (EAC, 2012). However, as highlighted by England et al. (2021) in the case of Kenyan fashion, there has been a tendency to focus on manufacturing rather than the creative component. It is important to note that DHK describes design as value addition to a product or service. Subsequently, it has positioned itself as a coworking hub where there is a confluence of a diverse mix of talented people from the creative class like animators, filmmakers, architects, health experts using creative solutions, advocates and policy content developers, as well as freelance clients. However, the value addition created at DHK is not directly aligned to Uganda's industrialisation agenda. In fact, as highlighted by Comunian and Kimera (2021) in relation to the Ugandan film and television sector, there is still very little investment in Uganda content development. In the case of CDEA some of the activities of the incubator are also aligned to value addition to the textile and leather value chains that are a priority in Tanzania's industrialisation agenda. However Tanzania's industrial sector for textile and leather products is guided by export-oriented industrial polices and not domestic markets, which is the target market for Tanzanian fashion designers, as in the case of Kenya, discussed by England et al. (2021). Therefore, there is a weak link between fashion designers and the Textile Development Unit Tanzania, whose target market for textile and apparel is international (Ministry of Industry and Trade Tanzania, 2000).

Urban development policies and creative agendas

While these initiatives add to democratising the space for creative hubs in East African cities, it appears that the emergence of coworking spaces and networks to facilitate CCI development is moving faster than cultural and urban policy development and has some setbacks. In the three East African cities, there are plans to redesign cities to fit the growing population and their spatial needs; however there is limited engagement with creative thinkers to capture the milieu of cultural spaces and coworking hubs within the master plans of future cities or expanding cities.

Despite the fact that the creative hubs in the three East African cities are not informed by a creative city policy, they respond to the needs of CCIs through the provision of coworking space, services to urban clients as well as space for creative expression and networking for the members of the hub and their clients. This illustrates how the creative hubs of Nairobi, Dar es Salaam and Kampala are localised in their urban cultural system of consumption and production. However, despite the merit in coworking hubs, the Covid-19 pandemic is a threat to the coworking model and presents the possibility of virtual coworking or the hybrid model (virtual and physical office) becoming a permanent fixture of the knowledge economy.

Urban development and creative hubs often have more to do with protecting local cultures and heritage (discussed below) but do not always allow for this connection to be made. With respect to Tanzania, urban development issues and policies are captured in the National Human Settlement Policy (Tanzania Ministry of Lands and Human Settlement Development, 2000).

National cultural policies and placemaking

Evans (2009), in an international study which included Africa, analysed CCI policies and strategies, based on a survey of public-sector creative city initiatives and plans and their underlying rationales. The study indicates that policy convergence is manifested by the promotion of creative spaces and industry clusters and versions of the digital media, however, using old industrial economic interventions and policy rationales. Evans states that cities are "utilizing the creative quarter/knowledge hub as a panacea to implement broader city expansion and regeneration plans" (ibid., 1003). Similarly, an analysis of cultural policy for Uganda (Uganda Ministry of Gender, Labour and Social Development, 2006) as well the Uganda National Urban Policy (Uganda Ministry of Trade, Industry & Cooperatives, 2017) shows a policy convergence within Policy Statement 8, aiming to create a conducive environment for investment in urban areas, that has strategies that could provide policy support for coworking hubs in Kampala. This also mentions: "ensure provision of public open spaces, promotion of urban tourism and cultural heritage as well as urban renewal and regeneration, and promotion of a healthy and safe urban environment" (ibid., iv).

Indeed, DHK is an example of a coworking hub that has not yet benefited from these policy incentives. However, because of the generic push for innovation which has become a buzz word in Uganda and a big movement for "Buy Uganda, Build Uganda" (BUBU), this has contributed to the growing need for creative product developers and the coworking space that stimulate collaborative design.

Despite the weak correlation between cultural and urban polices in Uganda, Kenya's cultural policy (Government of Kenya, 2009) also reflects policy correlation in commitment for the government to protect and promote Kenyan contemporary architecture through strategic urban planning, which contributes to a culturally adapted physical environment for a growing part of the Kenyan people. At county level, Nairobi County has legislation in place on arts and culture, though this needs further development to fully recognise the particularity of CCIs in the urban sphere. As a result, the GoDown Centre is located within the sustainable urban development agenda of Nairobi County to advocate for the intrinsic value of culture and other values in identity formation of the city. In 2013, the GoDown Centre contributed input to the Nairobi Integrated Urban Development Master Plan.

Finally, with respect to Tanzania, urban development issues and policies are captured in the National Human Settlement Policy (Tanzania Ministry of Lands and Human Settlement Development, 2000). However, there is no direct correlation with the Tanzania Cultural Policy (1997) that can anchor the establishment of coworking hubs or creative spaces. This could also be because the cultural policy of Tanzania is still under review.

Challenges and opportunities for creative hubs

The case studies presented and their connection (and disconnection) with national industrial policies suggest that there is often a narrow linkage between the industrialisation agenda and creative hubs in East African cities within a too narrow focus on the agro processing, glass products and cosmetics value chains (EAC, 2012). Furthermore, correlation between the cultural and urban policy is non-existent in Kenya since strategies for creativity, innovation and heritage are still in draft form, while Tanzanian cultural and urban policies do not have any correlation. For Uganda, the urban policy has a strategy for the provision of incentives for innovation and creativity and the creation of business incubators to propel urban economic growth; however, implementation is yet to take place.

Yet, policy formulation and review require constant vigilance and advocacy from groups like the Creative Economy Working Group in Kenya and the newly established Uganda Cultural and Creative Industries Forum and Creative Industries Network Tanzania. However, governments move slowly, and so an enabling framework for creative hubs in urban areas is partially actualised in Kenya through the Nairobi County, but not yet achieved for Uganda and Tanzania. As a result, coworking hubs for CCIs in East African cities have had to push ahead of policy to find solutions for the urban development agenda.

While the fourth industrial revolution presents an opportunity for the East African economies to leapfrog the traditional manufacturing-based economy into the knowledge economy, none of the three countries has prioritised media and digital industries for value addition. This is a missed opportunity for creative hubs to play a pivotal role in co-creating innovative solutions for social impact. Yet, in Nairobi technology innovation has given rise to the development of the Konza city project (Van Noorloos et al., 2019), while in Dar es Salaam, the tech industry stakeholders are pushing for the establishment of Silicon Dar; this is an area that is organically developing into a tech cluster as a result of hosting a number of telecommunication companies and start-up tech companies in one location.

While policy formulation and review can be slow and tedious, and often times narrows the space for CCIs in urban development, policy is still necessary to provide a framework for creative hubs to contribute towards urban and national development. The alternative solution should be to focus on strategy rather than policy, while at the same time developing evidence for the need to link CCIs in urban and industrialisation policies. For instance, the three creative coworking spaces could host creative city dialogues on topics that involve the creative class and showcasing the role of CCIs in urban renewal and regeneration and the industrialisation agenda.

From this analysis it is important to consider how creative hubs can connect not only with local urban policies but also with a broader national agenda in relation to national industrial policy and also national cultural policy (Figure 7.6).

In addition, coworking hubs can become nodes for proof of concept for CCIs in light industrial value addition through content development for television and digital platforms, design for textile and leather industries and eco products like cosmetics and furniture targeting domestic, regional and the sustainable tourism market.

It is therefore easy to argue for the importance of creative hubs in Africa and more specifically in the three East African cities we analysed.

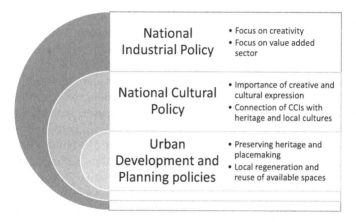

Figure 7.6 Creative hubs connecting across policy scales and agendas.
Note: CCIs, cultural and creative industries.

City authorities that are developing tech districts in their new city master plans, like Nairobi and Dar es Salaam, should locate media and digital industry coworking spaces within the tech districts so as to stimulate collaborative design. Adopting a clustering approach for creative hubs in the old industrial areas will stimulate urban renewal and revitalisation initiatives for the sustainability of urban areas. Furthermore, bridging consumption and production (Cunningham, 2012), creative hubs could also connect with the development of recreational and cultural facilities in urban policies or city master plans that are aligned to the tourism value chain.

Conclusion

This chapter has illustrated that there is a narrow linkage between the industrialisation agenda and creative hubs in the context of East African cities within their manufacturing and agricultural-focused production chains. In addition, there is no correlation between cultural and urban polices since the Kenyan urban policy, that has strategies for creativity, innovation, recreational and cultural facilities and heritage, is still in draft form, while Tanzanian cultural and urban policies do not have any correlation. For Uganda, the urban policy has a strategy for the provision of incentives for innovation and creativity and the creation of business incubators to propel urban economic growth; however, implementation is yet to take place.

The arguments presented highlight that creative hubs in East African cities have existed outside policy guidance. It is important for their existence and activities to be anchored within urban policies and city master plans to enhance sustainable development. Furthermore, as we write this chapter the Covid-19 pandemic still heavily influences further planning and work, so it is important to consider how creative hubs in East Africa can survive and ride the changes and new challenges ahead. It is possible that virtual coworking will become a permanent fixture of the knowledge economy; this resonates with Johns and Gratton (2013), who argue that digitalising the mode of production enables work to be performed anywhere at any time. However, there is also evidence that Covid-19 will affect many creative workers and freelancers who cannot rely on a stable income or business model (Comunian and England, 2020). Nevertheless, even within this challenging context ahead, creative hubs could become key and instrumental to offer support and a collaborative environment for African cities to re-think their post-Covid-19 future and for urban and national policies to coordinate further their agenda with the creative economy.

References

Botsman R. and Rogers R. (2011) *What's Mine Is Yours: How Collaborative Consumption is Changing the Way we Live*. London: Collins.

British Council (2013) *Scoping the Creative Economy in East Africa*. Available at: www.britishcouncil.org/east-africa-arts/research/creative-economy (accessed 06/08/2020).

British Council (2015) *Creative Hub Toolkit*. Available at: http://creativeconomy. britishcouncil.org/blog/15/06/28/creative-hubkitmade-hubs-emerging-hubs (accessed 06/08/2020).

Capdevila I. (2013) Knowledge Dynamics in Localized Communities: Coworking Spaces as Microclusters. Available at SSRN 2414121 (accessed 10/06/2020).

Chapain C.A. and Comunian R. (2010) Enabling and inhibiting the creative economy: the role of the local and regional dimensions in England. *Regional Studies* 43(6): 717–734.

Chatterton P. (2000) Will the real creative city please stand up? *City* 4(3): 390–397.

Comunian R. and England L. (2020) Creative and cultural work without filters: Covid-19 and exposed precarity in the creative economy. *Cultural Trends* 29(2): 112–128.

Comunian R. and Kimera G. (2021) Uganda film and television: creative skills development and skills gap for the sector. In: Comunian R., Hracs B.J. and

England L. (eds) *Higher Education and Policy for Creative Economies in Africa*. London: Routledge, pp. 44–59.

Comunian R., Chapain C. and Clifton N. (2010) Location, location, location: exploring the complex relationship between creative industries and place. *Creative Industries Journal* 3: 5–10.

Cunningham S. (2012) The creative cities discourse: production and/or consumption. *Cities, Cultural Policy and Governance* 111–121.

De Jong V. (2017) *Design Hub Kampala*. Available at: www.theurbandetective. com/blogs/2017/6/12/design-hub-kampala (accessed 06/08/2020).

Dovey J., Pratt A., Lansdowne J., Moreton, S., Virani, T. and Merkel, J. (2016) *Creative Hubs: Understanding the New Economy*. Available at: http://qmro. qmul.ac.uk/xmlui/handle/123456789/25419 (accessed 06/08/2020).

EAC (2012) *The East African Community Industrialization Policy in Brief*. Available at: https://eacgermany.org/wp-content/uploads/2014/10/EAC-Industrialization-Policy-Brief.pdf (accessed 13/08/2020).

England L., Mosomi O., Comunian R. and Hracs B. J. (2021) Fashion designers and education in Nairobi: challenges and opportunities. In: Comunian R., Hracs B.J. and England L. (eds) *Higher Education and Policy for Creative Economies in Africa*. London: Routledge.

Evans G. (2009) Creative cities, creative spaces and urban policy. *Urban Studies* 46(5–6): 1003–1040.

Florida R. (2002) *The Rise of the Creative Class*. New York: Basic Books.

Gandini A. (2015) The rise of coworking spaces: a literature review. *ephemera* 15(1): 193.

GoDown Arts Centre (2020) LinkedIn Profile. Available at: www.linkedin.com/ company/godownarts/?originalSubdomain=ke (accessed 06/08/2020).

Government of Kenya (2009) *National Policy on Culture and Heritage*. Available at: https://en.unesco.org/creativity/sites/creativity/files/activities/conv2005_ eu_docs_kenya_policy.pdf (accessed 13/08/2020).

Hayden C. and Ball-Rokeach S.J. (2007) Maintaining the digital hub: locating the community technology center in a communication infrastructure. *New Media and Society* 9(2): 235–257.

Johns T. and Gratton L. (2013) The third wave of virtual work. *Harvard Business Review* 91(1): 66–73.

KCCA (2003) *The National Environment (Noise Standards and Control) Regulations, 2003 (Under Sections 28 and 107 of the National Environment Act Cap 153)*. Available at: www.kcca.go.ug/uploads/acts/Noise%20 Standards%20and%20Control%20Regulations.pdf (accessed 13/08/2020).

Kenya Ministry of Industrialization (2012) *Sessional Paper No. 9 of 2012 on the National Industrialization Policy*. Available at: www.industrialization. go.ke/images/downloads/policies/the-national-industrialization-policy.pdf (accessed 12/08/2020).

Lee C.-H., Ro H.-B. and Tcha D.-W. (1993) Topological design of a two-level network with ring-star configuration. *Computers and Operations Research* 20(6): 625–637.

Leforestier A. (2009) *The Co-Working Space Concept.* Available at: http://salus. adapt.it/wp-content/uploads/2020/04/LEFORESTIER_Co-working-space_ 2009.pdf (accessed 06/08/2020).

Luo Y. and Chan R.C. (2020) Production of coworking spaces: evidence from Shenzhen, China. *Geoforum* 110: 97–105.

Merkel J. (2015) Coworking in the city. *ephemera* 15(2): 121–139.

Ministry of Industry and Trade Tanzania (2000) *Textile Development Unit Tanzania.* Available at: https://tdu.or.tz/investing-in-tanzania/ (accessed 06/ 08/2020).

Moriset B. (2013) *Building New Places of the Creative Economy. The Rise of Coworking Spaces.* Available at: https://halshs.archives-ouvertes.fr/halshs-00914075/document (accessed 21/07/2020).

Rantisi N.M (2002) The local innovation system as a source of variety: openness and adaptability in New York City's Garment District. *Regional Studies: The Journal of the Regional Studies Association* 587–602.

Reed B. (2007) *Co-Working: The Ultimate in Teleworking Flexibility.* Available at: www.networkworld.com/article/2287504/co-working--the-ultimate-in-teleworking-flexibility.html (accessed 06/08/2020).

Rusk M. (2011) Design thinking, enterprise and innovation: strategies for stimulating creative hubs and making an impact on city regeneration. In: *Design Management: Toward a new era of innovation.* Hong Kong: Innovation and Design Management Association, pp. 20–27.

Sedini C., Vignati A. and Zurlo F. (2014) Conceiving a (new) definition of hub for the development of a transnational network for creative companies. In: Wiktor-Mach, D. and Radwański, P. (eds) *The Idea of Creative City/The Urban Policy Debate*, 106–118.

Shiach M., Nakano D., Virani T., et al. (2017) Report on creative hubs and urban development goals (UK/Brazil). *Creative Hubs and Urban Development Goals (UK/Brazil).* São Paulo: Carlos Alberto Vanzolini Foundation

Spinuzzi C. (2012) Working alone together: coworking as emergent collaborative activity. *Journal of Business and Technical Communication* 26(4): 399–441.

Tanzania Ministry of Lands and Human Settlement Development (2000) *National Human Settlement Policy.* Available at: www.tzonline.org/pdf/ nationalhumansettlements.pdf (accessed 06/08/2020).

Tanzania Ministry of Trade and Industry (1997) *Sustainable Industries Development Policy SIDP (1996–2020).* Available at: www.tzonline.org/pdf/ sustainableindustrial.pdf (accessed 13/08/2020).

Tintiangko J and Soriano CR (2020) Coworking spaces in the Global South: local articulations and imaginaries. *Journal of Urban Technology* 27(1): 67–85.

Uganda Ministry of Gender, Labour and Social Development (2006) *The Uganda National Culture Policy.* Available at: https://ocpa.irmo.hr/resources/ policy/Uganda_Culture_Policy-en.pdf (accessed 13/08/2020).

Uganda Ministry of Trade, Industry & Cooperatives (2017) *National Industrial Policy.* Available at: www.tralac.org/files/2012/12/Uganda_National-Industrial-Policy.pdf (accessed 13/08/2020).

UNDP and UNESCO (2013) Creative Economy Report: Widening Local Development Pathways. Paris: UNDP/UNESCO.

Van Noorloos F., Avianto D. and Opiyo R.O. (2019) New master-planned cities and local land rights: the case of Konza Techno City, Kenya. *Built Environment* 44(4): 420–437.

Waters-Lynch J, Potts J, Butcher T, Dodson, J. and Hurley J. (2016) Coworking: A Transdisciplinary Overview. Available at SSRN: https://ssrn.com/abstract=2712217. (Accessed 13/08/2020).

Part III

Clustering and creative spaces

8 Rural cultural and creative industry clustering

The Sarah Baartman District, South Africa

Fiona Drummond and Jen Snowball

Introduction

It is increasingly recognised that the cultural and creative industries (CCIs) can play an important role in economic growth and development. The socio-economic development potential of the CCIs has been widely acknowledged amongst developed countries since the 1990s (Flew and Cunningham, 2010). Moreover, traditional theory states that, for the CCIs to promote development, they should form clusters in large metropolitan centres where they can take advantage of the various hard and soft infrastructures that the creative city has to offer (Florida, 2002; Landry, 2008). Accordingly, the majority of academic research into the CCIs has centred around cities in developed countries. However, the urban bias is starting to be addressed as there have been several case studies in developed countries like Australia, the United Kingdom, the United States and Scandinavia which have found cultural and creative clusters in non-metropolitan spaces.

Relatively recently, developing countries like South Africa have been implementing specific cultural development policies at the regional level that are aimed at growing the CCIs to foster economic growth and local economic development (LED). This is a response to issues of unemployment, poverty and inequality that have resulted from a phase of economic decline in rural South Africa due to the contraction of their former economic mainstays: agriculture, mining and railways (Hoogendoorn and Nel, 2012). In an attempt to address these issues, many small towns have adopted post-productivist strategies in which consumption-based activities like lifestyle, leisure and tourism become economic goods (Hoogendoorn and Nel, 2012). Following the global trend, policy, investment and research have tended to focus on the country's large cities like Johannesburg and Cape Town. This study helps to address both the developed country and urban biases within

DOI: 10.4324/9781003191681-8

research on creative economies by investigating CCI clustering in a rural, small-town context in the developing country of South Africa.

Context and theory: the Sarah Baartman District and CCI clustering

The Sarah Baartman District (SBD) (Figure 8.1) is predominantly rural with no large urban centres. This small and sparse settlement pattern can be explained by the combination of the district's vast area, land cover (nature conservation areas) and land use (extensive agriculture). Though improvements have been made to living conditions, with most people living in formal housing with access to piped water and electricity, the district faces issues of low economic growth (3,41%), high unemployment (17,8%), low education levels (35% of people over the age of 20 have completed secondary school) as well as high poverty and inequality (Statistics South Africa, 2016). Conventional theory suggests that CCIs cluster in areas with higher economic growth rates, skilled labour pools, access to technology and relatively wealthy populations (including the creative class) to act as consumers (Florida, 2002; Landry, 2008). Therefore, according to the dominant body of literature, the SBD is not well suited to the clustering of CCIs. Despite this, local

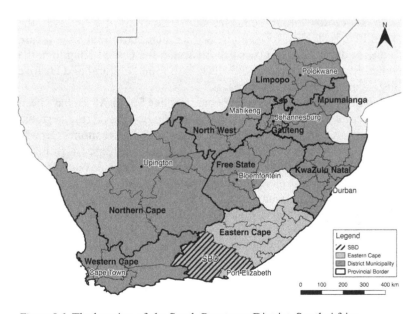

Figure 8.1 The location of the Sarah Baartman District, South Africa.

government has identified culture as having a strong regional development potential based on history, festivals, fine arts and crafts and natural heritage (Sarah Baartman District Municipality, 2017).

The interest in harnessing the CCIs as a new economic growth driver stems from the post-productivist shift that has occurred across small-town South Africa in response to the contraction of the former economic mainstays which have resulted in problems of stagnating economies, severe unemployment and poverty (Hoogendoorn and Visser, 2016). In accordance with post-productivism, to combat these issues small towns and rural areas need to identify new development opportunities, the most successful of which have relied on the characteristics of the town that make it special rather than the rural hinterland (Hoogendoorn and Nel, 2012). This relates to sense of place and local characteristics, including cultural, historical and physical assets. Therefore, many small towns, including some within the SBD, are pursuing culture-led development, mainly through tourism initiatives (Hoogendoorn and Visser, 2016). It is thus hoped that the CCIs will be part of the solution to the problems that affect small towns in a manner that Florida suggests: attracting the creative class (either permanently or as visitors) will result in job creation and economic growth with the direct and spill-over benefits associated with the CCIs being multiplied throughout the economy.

Despite local government's recognition of the developmental potential of culture, there are only a few policy initiatives that directly target the CCIs, including financial support to festivals and some CCI businesses as well as attempts to establish agri-tourism routes with a CCI element (Sarah Baartman District Municipality, 2017). Most policies are more generalised, but will also benefit the CCIs. Such policies include tourism development, improving education and skills development, supporting small and micro-enterprises (defined as having ten or fewer employees – a category that many CCI businesses fall under), upgrading telecommunications (especially broadband), regenerating core towns (though not specified, this could be done by developing cultural precincts or clusters) and by building regional networks (Sarah Baartman District Municipality, 2017). Though these policies will help the CCIs, it is not enough to propel the sector forward so that it can have the desired impacts on economic growth and job creation. A specialised regional cultural policy is required for the sector to thrive. The first steps in formulating this policy involve conducting a fine-scale CCI-mapping audit study of the SBD to identify where CCIs are operating, whether they are clustering and which domains are prominent and may have a comparative advantage (Ndhlovu, 2017).

Research methods

Though there are a number of definitions of CCIs, this study utilised the United Nations Educational, Scientific and Cultural Organisation (UNESCO) (2009) Framework for Cultural Statistics (FCS) definition because it allows for international comparisons and is increasingly being used in South African policy documents. The FCS identifies six main domains: cultural and natural heritage, performance and celebration, visual arts and crafts, books and press, audio-visual and interactive media, and design and creative services. They include both the more traditional sectors (such as music, fine art, film and literature) and more commercial applications (such as architecture, design and advertising). However, this study did not include natural heritage (such as nature reserves) as it is not usually considered as a part of the cultural sector in South Africa and is governed by a separate body.

In order to identify which CCIs are present in the district and whether clusters have formed, a fine-scale audit of CCI businesses operating within the district was conducted in 2017. This built on two previous studies (Department of Arts and Culture, 2014; Lankester et al., 2016) which were not as extensive. The first phase of the research included internet searches of tourism-related sites and online business directories; the collection of local business directories and tourism brochures listing CCI-related tourist attractions like museums, galleries and craft markets and the use of Google Earth and Street View to conduct virtual searches of the towns. Many of the SBD towns and municipalities are pursuing tourism strategies in line with the post-productivist shift and so have created their own dedicated tourist brochures and websites. In total 46 local tourist brochures and websites were consulted, and seven local business directories were found. The brochures and websites covered all of the SBD municipalities, with those that were more invested in tourism as a development strategy having more brochures. The second phase involved field trips to the towns in order to verify the information already collected and to identify additional CCIs through snowball sampling and surveying the towns. Due to information on small towns being relatively limited, field research proved to be the most valuable technique of locating operational CCIs. Business name, goods and/or services provided, UNESCO domain, contact details and location were captured for each CCI business and historic site. The numbers of CCIs by UNESCO domain and municipality are shown in Table 8.1.

This method of conducting an audit of CCIs has resulted in the most accurate database of CCI businesses, their locations and activities to date for the SBD. The 2017 audit study found a total of 1,048 CCIs, double

Table 8.1 United Nations Educational, Scientific and Cultural Organisation (UNESCO) domain breakdown of the cultural and creative industries (CCIs) in the Sarah Baartman District (SBD)

Municipality	Domains					
	Cultural heritage	Performance and celebration	Visual arts and crafts	Books and press	Audio-visual and interactive media	Design and creative services
Baviaans	32	6	31	3	0	1
Blue Crane Route	23	2	19	8	0	2
Camdeboo	58	7	69	11	1	7
Ikwezi	12	0	8	2	0	1
Kouga	29	13	108	26	3	53
Kou-Kamma	6	1	21	4	0	0
Makana	53	51	75	26	7	21
Ndlambe	46	9	107	24	1	32
Sundays River Valley	4	3	11	9	0	2
SBD total	**263**	**92**	**449**	**113**	**12**	**119**

Source: Drummond and Snowball (2019).

that of the 2016 study and four times as many as the 2014 study. This illustrates the importance of conducting fine-scale research and that the method is effective and appropriate for rural small-town areas so can be implemented in other contexts. Accurate data is important for designing place-specific cultural policy based on CCI clustering and UNESCO domain activity as policies based on the earlier studies would have had different focus areas since the prominent domains differed across the clusters and so would have resulted in different policy outcomes.

Geographic information systems (GIS) can be a particularly useful component to include in research and analysis as it can take large data sets and display them in a simpler visual manner which makes interpretation easier and may bring to light relationships that were not previously highlighted in complex databases, tables and graphs. Though there have been many mapping studies of CCIs, it is not often that a geographic map is generated from the collected data. GIS can add value to creative economy research by examining how culture, creativity and spatiality interconnect and interact, which is especially pertinent to CCI clusters and creative cities (or creative small places) research as they are embedded within space (De Bernard et al., forthcoming). This research therefore included the production of geographic maps using ESRI's ArcGIS Desktop.

The first map investigates whether clustering is possible in small-town rural areas by using graduated circles, where a larger circle indicates the presence of a greater number of total CCIs. For the purposes of this research, a cluster was determined by the total number of CCIs in a town. This method has been used in other studies; for instance, a 2014 audit of Johannesburg's Maboneng precinct counted 44 CCIs across various UNESCO domains (Gregory, 2016). This logic was applied to the small-town context where the whole town is treated in a similar manner to a district or precinct in the city, given that CCIs tend to locate in the town centres (be that along the beachfront, main road or historic town centre). The second map analyses the breakdown of UNESCO domains within each town to identify the locations and domains of comparative advantage. This is reinforced by a location quotient (LQ) analysis for each domain per municipality. The LQ is calculated by dividing a municipality's percentage of CCIs in a given UNESCO domain by the percentage of all CCIs that the municipality has. If the result is greater than one, then the municipality can be said to have a comparative advantage in that particular domain.

Results: small-town clustering

While the District has a relatively large number of CCIs, they are not evenly distributed throughout the 35 towns and nine municipalities (Figure 8.2). Four categories of small-town CCI clusters in the SBD were identified: towns without clusters (below 20 CCIs); towns with clustering potential (between 20 and 34); and towns with clusters. Where CCI clusters were identified, they were split into two groups: those with small clusters (between 35 and 56) and those with large clusters (57 and above). The relationship between the number of CCIs and the socio-economic status of the municipality in which they are found is further discussed in Drummond and Snowball (2019). Very briefly, there was generally a positive relationship between a higher socio-economic status (a measure of welfare and access to basic services) and the presence of the CCIs. The analysis showed that there is likely to be a threshold level of socio-economic development that must be attained before CCI activity becomes significant.

In order to increase the probability of success, LED schemes based on the arts, culture and heritage sector would need to target the UNESCO domains which are well adapted to rural small-town environments and are prominent within the town or district so that they are building from an existing base (Oakley, 2006; Fleischmann et al., 2017). Figure 8.3

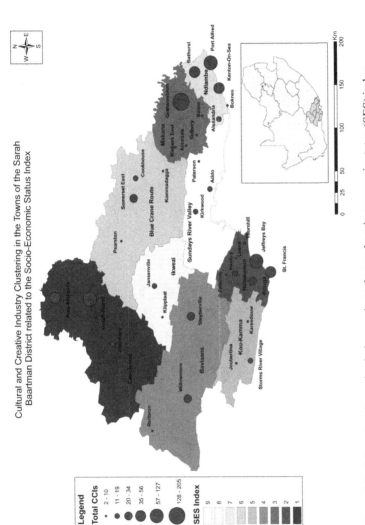

Figure 8.2 Cultural and creative industry clustering and socio-economic status (SES) index.

Note: CCIs, cultural and creative industries.

Source: Drummond and Snowball, 2019.

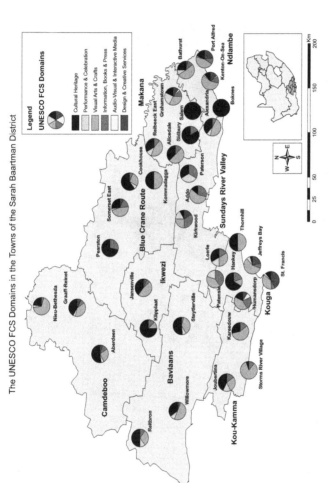

Figure 8.3 United Nations Educational, Scientific and Cultural Organisation (UNESCO) domain breakdown in the towns of the Sarah Baartman District (SBD).

Note: FCS, Framework for Cultural Statistics.

Source: Authors' own data and analysis.

Table 8.2 . Location quotients for the United Nations Educational, Scientific and Cultural Organisation (UNESCO) domains in the Sarah Baartman District (SBD) municipalities

Municipality	Cultural heritage	Performance and celebration	Visual arts and crafts	Books and press	Audio-visual and interactive media	Design and creative services
Baviaans	1.75	0.94	0.99	0.38	0.00	0.12
Blue Crane Route	1.70	0.42	0.82	1.37	0.00	0.33
Camdeboo	1.51	0.52	1.05	0.67	0.57	0.40
Ikwezi	2.08	0.00	0.81	0.81	0.00	0.38
Kouga	0.50	0.64	1.09	1.04	1.13	2.01
Kou-Kamma	0.75	0.36	1.53	1.16	0.00	0.00
Makana	0.91	2.49	0.75	1.03	2.62	0.79
Ndlambe	0.84	0.47	1.14	1.02	0.40	1.29
Sundays River Valley	0.55	1.18	0.89	2.88	0.00	0.61

Source: Authors' own data and analysis.

presents the UNESCO domain breakdowns while Table 8.2 provides the LQ analysis. A comparative advantage acts as a signal to policy and decision makers to invest in the particular domain in its location of advantage, be that the town, group of neighbouring towns, municipality or district as a whole.

Four interrelated dimensions of hard infrastructure, governance, soft infrastructure and markets determine the potential of urban and rural places to support the growth of the creative economy (Comunian et al., 2010). For rural places, the soft infrastructure of the wider region as well as individual CCI clusters in the small towns are important factors in CCI clustering and culture-led development as it is these softer idiosyncratic reasons like the place image, networks and traditions that make a place attractive to creative individuals who may establish businesses that capitalise on the local features and attract tourists to the area (Chapain and Comunian, 2010). Establishing a CCI cluster and creating policies to support its continued growth and development is desirable for the direct benefits of stimulating local economic growth and development and creating employment as well as indirect benefits of spillovers. The spillover effects of CCI clusters can be substantial and include knowledge spillovers, where new ideas developed by CCI businesses are applied elsewhere without compensation, product spillovers, where CCI goods and services increase the demand for complementary goods and services and network spillovers, where the presence of CCIs benefits other local firms by making the place more attractive and giving it a creative atmosphere (Chapain et al., 2010).

Having mapped the spatial distribution of the number and type of CCIs in the SBD, the results were then analysed according to the UNESCO domain activities as they provide the basis from which policies can be designed to develop the district's creative economy and CCI clusters.

Group 1: a strong presence in the SBD

The first group consists of the two domains with the strongest presence throughout the district: visual arts and crafts and cultural heritage. These two domains are the largest in the district, occurring in large proportions in most of the SBD towns. This is supported by the LQ results: in the case of visual arts and crafts, Camdeboo, Kouga, Kou-Kamma and Ndlambe have locational concentrations while Baviaans, Blue Crane Route, Camdeboo and Ikwezi have locational concentrations in cultural heritage.

Given its district-wide presence in large proportions, it seems that the SBD is particularly well suited to visual arts and crafts. This is due to some of the municipalities being popular tourist destinations as they include towns with historical, cultural and natural attractions (Sarah Baartman District Municipality, 2017). Tourism can have significant spillover effects on this domain through souvenir production for tourist markets linked to the specific characteristics of the town (Rogerson, 2010). For towns with CCI clustering potential like Stytlerville and Willowmore with small mohair agri-tourism industries, a part of the attraction is the visual arts and crafts products based on mohair, like handmade fashion and soft toys. There is an element of creative tourism within the SBD where the purpose of travel is to engage with and participate in arts and crafts activities so that the domain becomes an attraction in itself (Richards, 2019). Fieldwork revealed that towns like Bathurst and Nieu-Bethesda (small CCI clusters category) have reputations as artists' havens and creative spaces so that the artistic nature of the towns is a major factor in their CCI clustering and tourism attraction. Policy initiatives surrounding this domain could thus be linked to tourism development strategies as the strong links between them have been widely acknowledged (Rogerson, 2010).

The visual arts and crafts domain has been recognised for its socio-economic development potential and inclusivity due to its potential in creating job opportunities and income for previously disadvantaged and marginalised people, many of whom are women, as it is not necessary to have a formal education to be able to participate (Rogerson, 2010). Since the SBD has a relatively poorly educated population, high poverty rates and high unemployment rates, many people may have already turned towards this domain as a means of earning an income. Consequently, this is an especially good domain to invest in as, considering its inclusivity, LED schemes are more likely to help the poorer members of the SBD community.

The visual arts and crafts domain is strong throughout South Africa in terms of its share of cultural occupations, and so the SBD follows the national trend (Hadisi and Snowball, 2017). The domain has accordingly been identified as an industrial policy focus area and as a key manufacturing sector that is both value adding and labour intensive with a good potential for export (Department of Trade and Industry, 2013). The strength of the domain within the Eastern Cape has also been recognised in provincial cultural policy (Department of Sports, Recreation, Arts and Culture, 2018).

The prominence of cultural heritage is more problematic as the type of cultural heritage that is present is highly variable. All of the towns have monuments and historic sites but few of them have museums, art galleries or tours and information relating to the monuments and sites. In this sense, there is not a cluster of cultural heritage but rather a concentration of potential places of interest in the towns with large proportions of the domain. There is thus a developmental potential for cultural heritage as it is necessary to have existing sites of historical and cultural interest which can be turned into attractions and so harnessed for development. It is possible for cultural and historic sites to make a valuable economic contribution. Cultural heritage tourism represents an increasingly important development opportunity for African countries, which have rich and diverse cultural heritage (Fyanka and Nwoko, 2015). Recent data (UNCTAD, 2017) shows that international tourist arrivals to Africa grew at 6% per year between 1995 and 2014, with some countries (Egypt, South Africa and Morocco) recording more than nine million international tourist arrivals in 2015. Along with wildlife tourism, cultural tourism is one of the largest draw-cards. The total average contribution of tourism to the gross domestic product

(GDP) of African countries was 8.3% in 2015 (UNCTAD, 2017). The SBD audit found that there exists a diverse range of places of interest spanning settler and colonial history, Xhosa history, the Anglo-Boer wars and old churches and so there appears to be a good existing base from which to build. Therefore, cultural heritage has the potential to be a significant job creator and income generator if the necessary visitor infrastructure is put in place and the historic sites are well maintained and upgraded.

Given the district-wide prominence of the domain, a district-wide policy of maintaining and upgrading cultural heritage sites is recommended with the possibility of tourist routes for certain types of cultural heritage being developed. These tourist routes are based on the assets of a group of towns such as battlefield tourism surrounding the Anglo-Boer wars in Somerset East, Steytlerville and Willowmore; settler history in Bathurst, Grahamstown, Port Alfred and Salem; or historic church tourism throughout the district as almost every town has an architecturally beautiful old church. Accordingly, the management strategy for the cultural heritage domain will need to be district-led and so falls under the 'direction' cluster management strategy where the SBD municipality would need to collect and distribute funds and engage in considerable planning efforts (Brooks and Kushner, 2001). This recommendation is based on the likelihood of initiatives related to the domain being capable of benefiting several towns and municipalities.

Group 2: areas of comparative advantage

The second group is for domains that hold a comparative advantage according to the LQ analysis and includes design and creative services and performance and celebration. Design and creative services is the third largest domain yet occurs in less than half of the SBD towns with a comparative advantage in St Francis and Jeffreys Bay in Kouga and Kenton-On-Sea and Port Alfred in Ndlambe. There is thus a node of design and creative services activity in these four towns. The CCI audit found that interior design, landscaping and architecture were the prominent domain activities within the nodes. Field observations suggest that this activity may be the result of the four towns being popular holiday destinations with significant second-homeowner communities who have a relatively high demand for the services of property-related design and creative services businesses.

Since the design and creative services activity within the nodes is largely property-related, a potential LED policy initiative may be to link the domain to the property industry by encouraging new property developments (commercial and private) to use local architects, interior designers and landscapers. Hubs of property-related design and creative services could also be created. This suggests that cluster management should use the 'development' strategy whereby district leadership acts as a catalyst for private investment in forming these property development-related design and creative services clusters (Brooks and Kushner, 2001).

Performance and celebration is the second smallest domain in the SBD, with 92 CCIs occurring in 21 of the 35 towns. The performance and celebration domain is usually found in quite small proportions and in many of the towns takes the form of traditional dance groups and/or theatre groups. There is thus not much variety within the domain at the district level as only a handful of towns have different types of dance and music or host festivals. Grahamstown (Makhanda), which hosts the annual National Arts Festival and has a university (Rhodes University) as well as several schools, has a large number and wide variety of permanent performance and celebration CCIs which seem to be linked to and supported by these institutions. Moreover, in terms of comparative advantage, the LQ analysis shows that Makana has the strongest concentration of performance and celebration. Despite specialisation within the domain, there is no dedicated local policy to support the development of either artists or events.

Despite the lack of local government support, the provincial and district level governments have recognised the potential of the performance and celebration domain for development. There are a few existing developmental policies, including the promotion and support of district community arts development projects across several fields including dance, music and drama as well as financial support for one festival within the district a year with a focus on expanding the festival and nurturing local artists (Eastern Cape Provincial Arts and Culture Council, 2015; Lankester et al., 2016). The management of the performance and celebration domain links to the 'donation' cluster management strategy as it has mainly revolved around funding and some active planning (Brooks and Kushner, 2001). These are good starting points, but more needs to be done if the domain is to expand across the district.

Since design and creative services activity tends not to locate in the smaller and more agriculturally focused towns in large numbers, it is suggested that the domain is better suited to towns where there is a significant permanent and transient (tourist and second-homeowner community) consumer market. Furthermore, outside of the nodes, the main design and creative services activity is graphic design, which performed more of a support function to other businesses as it mostly existed in print shops. Thus, investing in this activity is unlikely to have much benefit at the district level. Therefore, it is not recommended for there to be investment in design and creative services outside of the nodes or towns that are characterised by more diverse domain activity combined with significant consumer markets. A more targeted policy approach is recommended which aims to capitalise on and strengthen the comparative advantage as this will expand the domain and thus reinforce any clustering activity.

However, this is not the case for performance and celebration as Bathurst and Nieu-Bethesda as well as the small, remote agricultural towns of Kirkwood and Loerie also hold festivals that would benefit from government investment and policy support. Moreover, establishing and supporting community centres that offer dance, music and theatre classes and performances would be a good social policy to introduce as it would contribute positively towards nation building and social cohesion as well as increasing involvement in the arts and promoting audience participation, thereby ensuring the future of the domain in the district.

Group 3: a limited presence in the SBD

The third group of domains includes books and press and audio-visual and interactive media which are not prominent in the district. There are 113 CCIs that are part of the books and press domain, making it the fourth largest in the district, with a presence in most of the towns. However, this presence, especially in the smaller, more agricultural towns, takes the form of small local libraries. The towns with more diverse economies and/or larger physical sizes have greater internal domain activity including book shops, local newspapers and publishers, although these are not present in large proportions. The LQ analysis and map results are thus not suggestive of comparative advantage or clustering but rather the roll-out of the Department of Arts and Culture's programme for the building and maintenance of libraries in all towns. This is supported by field observations of several recently built libraries in the district, especially in the smaller and more rural and remote towns.

Audio-visual and interactive media is by far the smallest domain in the district, with only 12 CCIs occurring across four towns (Graaff-Reinet, Humansdorp, Kenton-On-Sea and Grahamstown). Radio is the largest activity within the domain with a small amount of videography. According to the LQ analysis, Kouga and Makana have locational concentrations in this domain. However, when absolute advantage is considered, it is clear that there is no locational concentration or cluster as there are two and seven audio-visual and interactive media businesses respectively.

The very limited activity of these two domains in the SBD suggests that they are not well suited to rural small-town environments. For some activities in both domains (publishing and film and television production), this is because they require the hard and soft infrastructural advantages of cities. Rural small-town areas do not possess the same infrastructural advantages and so attracting domain activity away from the cities of Cape Town and Johannesburg, where it is currently located, would be highly unlikely. It is thus not recommended that these domain activities be heavily invested in as success is doubtful from a CCI development perspective, though there are social benefits attached to supporting library development. Furthermore, opportunity cost needs to be considered as investing in these domains means that the option of investing in the stronger domains that have a higher chance of benefiting more towns and people due to their greater presence is forgone.

Conclusion

In order for the CCIs to be a successful LED strategy, they need to have located in significant numbers, or clusters, within a town. This research thus helps to determine whether culture-led development is a viable strategy for small towns as, to increase the likelihood of success, a small town should have an existing CCI cluster from which to build and should focus on its UNESCO domain activities in which it holds a comparative advantage (Fleischmann et al., 2017). The fine-scale nature of the research, in terms of tracking the number and type of CCIs per town, shows how specific analysis (rather than broader trends) gives a richer understanding of rural creative economy activity. This kind of study is important for designing realistic and effective regional cultural policy that builds on existing comparative advantage and is place-specific, as not all types of CCI are suited to small-town operation, nor are they suited to every small town as each town's characteristics influence the type of CCI activity that occurs within it.

The relative UNESCO domain presence throughout the district provides insights into the nature of CCI clusters in small-town environments. For instance, the prominence of visual arts and crafts and cultural heritage and the limited presence of audio-visual and interactive media support the theory that domains that do not require specialist skills or equipment have a greater tendency to cluster in more rural areas (Oakley, 2006). The nodes of comparative advantage in design and creative services and performance and celebration also show that the type of CCI activity within a cluster is determined by the characteristics of the town, such as being popular holiday and second-homeowner destinations or hosting a major cultural event. It is these characteristics and UNESCO domain-clustering activities that should influence cultural policy as it capitalises on the existing assets of a small town and what makes it special.

The study also demonstrated how using GIS to produce geographic maps of CCI activity can facilitate analysis as it brought to light the spatial interconnections and interactions of CCI clustering and UNESCO domain activity within individual small towns, municipalities and the district as a whole. These relationships provide evidence-based policy implications for CCI planning which are place-specific rather than imported from cities and so are more likely to be successful. As suggested by De Bernard et al. (forthcoming), data organisation and visualisation in GIS allow for easy interpretation by the public so that technical barriers that hamper genuine community and government policy design, debate and engagement are reduced, andmore effective and inclusive cultural policy can be implemented.

References

Brooks A.C. and Kushner R.J. (2001) Cultural districts and urban development. *International Journal of Arts Management* 3(2): 4–15.

Chapain C.A. and Comunian R. (2010) Enabling or inhibiting the creative economy: the role of the local and regional dimensions in England. *Regional Studies* 44(6): 717–734.

Chapain C., Cooke P., De Propris L., MacNeill S. and Mateos-Garcia J. (2010) *Creative Clusters and Innovation: Putting Creativity on the Map.* London: NESTA.

Comunian R., Chapain C. and Clifton N. (2010) Location, location, location: exploring the complex relationship between creative industries and place. *Creative Industries Journal* 3(1): 5–10.

De Bernard M., Comunian R. and Vigano F. (forthcoming) On GIS and the creative economy: opportunities and challenges. In Comunian R., Faggian A., Heinonen J. and Wilson N. (eds) *A Modern Guide to the Creative Economy.* Cheltenham: Edward Elgar

Department of Arts and Culture (2014) *DAC National Mapping Study: Final Report.* Pretoria: Department of Arts and Culture.

Department of Sports, Recreation, Arts and Culture (2018) *Eastern Cape Department of Sport, Recreation, Arts and Culture.* Available at: www.ecsrac. gov.za/Pages/default.aspx (accessed 27/01/2018).

Department of Trade and Industry (2013) *Industrial Policy Action Plan 2013/ 14–2015/16.* Pretoria: Department of Trade and Industry.

Drummond F. and Snowball J. (2019) Cultural clusters as a local economic development strategy in rural small-town areas: Sarah Baartman District in South Africa. *Bulletin of Geography: Socio-Economic Series* 43: 107–119.

Eastern Cape Provincial Arts and Culture Council (2015) *Annual Report 2015*. Available at: https://provincialgovernment.co.za/entity_annual/157/2015-eastern-cape-eastern-cape-provincial-arts-and-culture-council-(ecpacc)-annual-report.pdf (accessed 28/01/2018).

Fleischmann K., Welters R. and Daniel R. (2017) Creative industries and regional economic development: can a creative industries hub spark new ways to grow a regional economy? *Australasian Journal of Regional Studies* 23(2): 217–242.

Flew T. and Cunningham S. (2010) Creative industries after the first decade of debate. *The Information Society* 26(2): 113–123.

Florida R. (2002) *The Rise of the Creative Class: And How it's Transforming Work, Leisure, Community and Everyday Life*. New York: Basic Books.

Fyanka B. and Nwoko K. (2015) Culture and tourism in modern Africa: an overview. In: Nwoko K. and Osiki O. (eds) *Dynamics of Culture and Tourism in Africa: Perspectives on Africa's Development in the 21st Century*. Ilishan-Remo, Nigeria: Babcock University Press, pp. 155–180.

Gregory J.J. (2016) Creative industries and urban regeneration – the Maboneng precinct, Johannesburg. *Local Economy* 31(1–2): 158–171.

Hadisi S. and Snowball J.D. (2017) *Employment in the Cultural and Creative Industries in South Africa*. Port Elizabeth: South African Cultural Observatory.

Hoogendoorn G. and Nel E. (2012) Exploring small town development dynamics in rural South Africa's post-productivist landscapes. In: Donaldson R. and Marais L. (eds) *Small Town Geographies in Africa: Experiences from South Africa and Elsewhere*. New York: Nova Science, pp. 21–34.

Hoogendoorn G. and Visser G. (2016) South Africa's small towns: a review on recent research. *Local Economy* 31(1–2): 95–108.

Landry C. (2008) *The Creative City: A Toolkit for Urban Innovators* (2nd edn). London: Earthscan.

Lankester T., Snowball J.D., Chippendale E. and Ndhlovu R. (2016) The cultural and creative industries in the Sarah Baartman Municipal District: development potential and cultural policy. Commissioned by the Sarah Baartman District Municipality Department of Arts and Culture. Grahamstown (Makhanda): National Arts Festival.

Ndhlovu R. (2017). The impact of the cultural and creative industries on the economic growth and development of small cities and towns – Guidelines for creating a regional cultural policy. Unpublished MCom Thesis. Grahamstown: Rhodes University.

Oakley K. (2006) Include us out – economic development and social policy in the creative industries. *Cultural Trends* 15(4): 255–273.

Richards G. (2019) Creative tourism: opportunities for smaller places? *Tourism and Management Studies* 15(SI): 7–10.

Rogerson C.M. (2010) The enterprise of craft: constraints and policy challenges in South Africa. *Acta Academia* 42(3): 115–144.

Sarah Baartman District Municipality (2017) *Sarah Baartman District Municipality Integrated Development Plan 2017–2022.* Available at: www. sarahbaartman.co.za/content/download/516 (accessed 28/01/2018).

Statistics South Africa (2016) *Community Survey 2016: In brief.* Available at: http://cs2016.statssa.gov.za/wp-content/uploads/2017/07/CS-in-brief-14-07-2017-with-cover_1.pdf (accessed 02/02/2018).

UNCTAD (2017) *Economic Development in Africa Report 2017: Tourism for Transformative and Inclusive Growth.* New York: United Nations.

UNESCO (2009) *2009 UNESCO Framework for Cultural Statistics.* Montreal: UNESCO Institute for Statistics.

9 The cultural centre of GugaS'thebe as a transformative creative space

Irma Booyens, Ndipiwe Mkuzo and Marco Brent Morgan

Introduction

Creativity is central to contemporary urban development and placemaking approaches, as also seen in South Africa and Cape Town more specifically (Duxbury et al., 2016; Minty and Nkula-Wenz, 2019; Oyekunle, 2017). In South Africa, as in other developing countries, the policy emphasis on culture is developmental, that is, employing culture as a resource for creative endeavours to open pathways for employment and poverty reduction, skills training and social upliftment (Duxbury et al., 2016; United Nations Conference on Trade and Development, 2011).

Moriset (2014) proposes that coworking spaces are the new places of the creative economy. A culture of coworking is evident at GugaS'thebe, a multi-purpose cultural space which is the anchor of an emerging creative and tourism precinct in Langa, a township on the periphery of Cape Town, South Africa. Townships are "marginalised areas on city or town fringes which emerged historically as a result of the segregation policies of South Africa's colonial and apartheid past" (Booyens and Rogerson, 2019a: 257). Booyens and Rogerson (2019a) identify creative experiences, spaces and events in Langa as examples of creative tourism and creative precinct development. This observation corresponds with recent work in South Africa which demonstrates that creative activities do not only cluster in larger urban areas, often inner-city areas, as the early creative city literature suggests, but are also found in peripheral urban areas, smaller cities and even in rural areas (Booyens and Rogerson, 2015; Drummond and Snowball, 2019; Gregory and Rogerson, 2018).

This chapter draws on site visits to GugaS'thebe and a focus group discussion with creative workers at the centre (*n* = 13) in June 2019. In addition, one of the authors worked for the Arts and Culture

DOI: 10.4324/9781003191681-9

Department in the City of Cape Town overseeing GugaS'thebe and other cultural spaces in townships. We argue that GugaS'thebe is a transformative space which not only serves as a cultural production space, but also stimulates social development. The structure of this chapter is as follows. In the second section, we situate townships as creative places and consider the literature on coworking spaces. In the third section we discuss the history of Langa and the case of GugaS'thebe as a transformative creative space. This is followed by our conclusions in the fourth section.

Literature

Townships as creative places

South Africa's townships are considered to be culturally vibrant in terms of arts, music and entertainment and leisure. Indeed, Jürgens and Donaldson (2012) observe that townships are repositioning themselves as niche markets for leisure and tourism on the pleasure periphery of cities. This, however, is not evident in all townships, but specifically in townships with rich heritage, particularly in terms of heritage associated with the struggle against apartheid, and especially in townships located close to large cities frequented by international visitors (Booyens, 2010).

At the same time, the multiple and multi-dimensional social and developmental challenges in townships dominate the literature (George and Booyens, 2014; Jürgens and Donaldson, 2012). One critical concern which is receiving increasing policy attention is the lack of economic opportunities in townships, historically designed as dormitory settlements rather than fully functional places (Booyens and Rogerson, 2019a; George and Booyens, 2014; Jürgens and Donaldson, 2012). Creativity arguably holds potential in townships for stimulating entrepreneurship, placemaking and physical upgrading (Booyens and Rogerson, 2019a, 2019b). This is based on observations that creative experiences and spaces linked to cultural heritage and tourism are emerging in townships and that there is a perceived latent visitor demand for this (Booyens and Rogerson, 2015, 2019a; George and Booyens, 2014).

The emphasis on creativity for township redevelopment and upgrading is theoretically underpinned by Southern urbanism notions which underscore that cities in the Global South should not merely be seen as places characterised by poverty and misery, but instead should also be recognised as places which exhibit a certain dynamism, vibrancy, resourcefulness, culture and also creativity (Choplin, 2016; Dovey and King, 2012; Frenzel, 2016, Pieterse, 2011). While Choplin (2016) cautions against an "over-romanticisation" of the creative capabilities in precarious neighbourhoods, Frenzel (2016) stresses that there is a real need to seek solutions for pressing social issues which include the stimulation of economic opportunities in these areas. One recommended area for creative economic diversification in townships is the establishment or expansion of multi-purpose cultural centres which can also serve as anchors for tourism precincts (Booyens and Rogerson, 2019a). Indeed, tourism can be regarded as a driver and demand generator for the creative economy since the consumers of creative products often are tourists (Adamo et al., 2019; Richards, 2018).

Coworking spaces

Gandini (2015: 194) describes coworking spaces as: "shared work places utilised by different sorts of knowledge professionals, mostly freelancers, working in various degrees of specialisation in the vast domain of the knowledge industry". These typically consist of shared office spaces utilised by independent professionals who hire a desk, Wi-Fi connection and some shared facilities (Gandini, 2015). Spaces tend to be small-scale initiatives founded by locals, who have strong connections and commitments to their localities, for use by local workers – knowledge and creative workers alike (Brown, 2017; Gandini, 2015). The nature of work is casual, project-based and rather precarious, as is characteristic of creative work (Brown, 2017; Gandini, 2015). The self-organising character of workers involved also comes to the fore in the literature (Brown, 2017). Gandini (2015) underscores that coworking spaces not only are hubs, but also act as relational milieus. Personal networks and social capital appear to be integral to the working of these spaces and the success of individuals (Brown, 2017; Gandini, 2015).

Moriset (2014) observes that coworking spaces emerged worldwide in the late 2000s as a new kind of workplace, initially as private initiatives, but the model has since been incorporated into public programmes for creative city making. There are also examples of not-for-profit organisations (NPOs) and semi-public spaces (Brown, 2017). The policy expectations are that these spaces can stimulate placemaking and neighbourhood renewal (Brown, 2017). Related models are innovation or business labs/hubs/incubators where the emphasis is often on digital and/or information technologies (Brown, 2017). Another more creative model is makerspaces which provide community-based workshops for designers to access shared technologies for digital design and fabrications (Smith, 2017). Smith (2017) argues that makerspaces can stimulate transformational social innovation. Makerspaces have lower entry barriers and are typically more open and democratic than other kinds of coworking spaces which can be seen as exclusionary. Smith (2017: 2) avers that, while makerspaces frequently "involve people experimenting and exploring technologies in playful ways", certain projects may "generate awareness of social implications, and be carried through to other areas of social life to attain wider significance for social development".

The case of GugaS'thebe

History and development of GugaS'thebe: embedded in culture and heritage

GugaS'thebe is situated in the township of Langa, located 11 km south-east of the centre of Cape Town. The township was established in 1927 on the site of the former Ndabeni "location". Langa township was named after King Langalibalele of the amaHlubi nation who was banished to Robben Island in 1874 for his rebellion against the British Colonial regime because he refused to register the rifles of his people (Giliomee and Mbenga, 2007). Upon sustained protest for his release, Langalibalele was eventually confined to a farm called Uitvlugt, which would later form part of Ndabeni location in 1901 and is remembered as "Langalibalele's location". Both Ndabeni and Langa were established as a result of segregation planning at the beginning of the 20th century.

Coetzer (2009) has suggested that the building of both Ndabeni and Langa was informed by a draft agreement developed by the Native Commission for Cape Town in 1900, which outlined plans to build a native location and gradually shift all "natives" or blacks from the inner city. According to Coetzer (2009), the agreement outlined a "native classification model" which categorised "natives" into three classes: those whom the city considered (1) temporary or migratory; (2) permanent or settled; or (3) educated and therefore "superior". It also proposed two typologies of accommodation to cater for the various "classes" of "natives" identified. For those deemed "stable natives" with families, a few small cottages were to be built; and for those considered "migratory natives", barracks or hostels would be built (Coetzer 2009). Locations were designed as "dormitory" settlements workers who often were migrants were meant to sleep in locations and work in the city during the day. Pass laws governed the movement of "natives" between town and township during different periods of the day. These dormitory settlements received limited infrastructure and services, designed only to accommodate in urban areas "temporary people" whose "homes" were meant to be in the "homelands" or "bantustans", and business development in these spaces was limited by legislation (Beavon and Rogerson 1990; Booyens and Rogerson 2019b).

The township of Langa emerged as a place of great resistance against apartheid. Apartheid was South Africa's system of racial segregation underscored by an oppressive and fascistic form of white nationalism. Apartheid policies were formally implemented though incremental laws and restrictions by the National Party after they came to power in 1948 and it continued until it was dissolved by the first democratic elections in 1994. In 1954, in protest against apartheid policies, thousands of Langa residents converged on the corner of Washington and Church Streets to burn their pass books before marching to town. On 21 March 1960, Langa residents reignited their commitment to liberation and marched under the leadership of the Pan Africanist Congress of Azania (PAC) in response to Robert Mangaliso Sobukwe's call to action against pass laws, which resulted in the Langa killings of 1960 when apartheid police gunned down protestors for refusing to disperse.

The GugaS'thebe cultural centre is currently located on the site where Langa residents gathered in protest against the pass laws. The centre was built in 1999, as a self-initiated, community-driven project focused on the cultural heritage of Southern Nguni Xhosa people. The centre is the anchor of the Langa cultural precinct which includes heritage sites like the Langa Pass Office Museum and the Old Post Office Museum. Aptly named GugaS'thebe, the cultural space derives its name from the Xhosa idiom *GugaS'thebe Kudala Usophulela*, which praises an ageing grass mat (*Isithebe*) used for its persisting service. Langa has a distinct sense of place captured visually by murals and mosaics spread throughout the township, depicting struggle heritage, migrant labour histories, the faces of well-known personalities from the area and contemporary culture. The GugaS'thebe space is vibrantly and richly decorated by the work of local artists (Figure 9.1). Street art images also depict the diversity and complexity of rural–urban migration flows and the emergent urban identities that produced the space (Figure 9.2). Migrant resistance against apartheid's forced-removal programme and racial segregationist spatial planning narratives are etched into the rich history and narrative of the place. Murals of the 1960s' anti-pass campaign were painted on the walls of the single-sex migrant hostels (now converted into flats) from the 1920s (Figure 9.2, left).

GugaS'thebe was initially imagined by the City of Cape Town as an incubator space for emerging artists and crafters. Following the collapse of GugaS'thebe Executive Committee in 2007, the management of the centre was transferred to the City of Cape Town's Arts and Culture

Figure 9.1 Street-front view of GugaS'thebe.

Figure 9.2 Murals on former men's hostels. Left: pass law protests; right: village and city life drawing on the theme of migration.

Branch. A series of studies were undertaken during the 2012–2013 period to inform the reimagining of the cultural precinct, including plans for significant capital investments toward improving tourist appeal, creating a space for people to develop their arts and to celebrate their heritage and culture (City of Cape Town, 2016). Today the centre is a vibrant cultural facility which supports local artists in their cultural production, as well as providing a platform for the sale of arts and crafts, cultural exchange, coworking and learning. Makerspaces at the centre engage a diverse group of crafters, artists and designers who share workshops or studios for the production of creative goods. A number of community-based organisations and NPOs like the GugaS'thebe Crafters Association, the Langa Arts Association, the Langa Heritage Foundation, Ombonwethu and Our Workshop constitute a collective of creatives and social entrepreneurs who act as intermediaries for artists and crafters alike. Although individuals or groups lease workshops or market spaces from the City on a monthly basis, there is a strong sense of ownership of the centre by local crafters, artists and designers. The space currently accommodates a range of creative endeavours, i.e. mosaic art (Figure 9.3), ceramics, painting, textiles (sewing), beading and weaving, performance art (dancing, drumming, theatre) and wire craft. The centre was expanded in 2014 to include the award-winning GugaS'thebe children's theatre, a space that has since attracted a variety of users which use it as a venue for events. The centre is often the

Figure 9.3 Mosaic artist at work in the studio he shares with a painter.

meeting point for walking tours and township experiences and has become a main feature for tourists visiting Langa.

While there are initiatives focused on youth skills training and development, the space is intergenerational. The diversity of the occupants creates the possibility of a meaningful interaction and collaboration between artists and crafters. There is a strong sense among creative workers at the space that they are there to stay as permanent tenants rather than "incubatees" who need to transition to somewhere else. This creates stability and ownership and contributes to the sustainability of the initiatives. This said, the young people who participated in our focus group do want to grow their businesses and some do have aspirations to move their operations elsewhere and expand their market into the greater Cape Town area. Some said they started with a home-based business and are now in a shared makerspace, but they want to grow and move out. GugaS'thebe accordingly is a "stepping stone" for them. Conversely, older crafters see themselves as mentors for up-and-coming young entrepreneurs. This suggests that "incubation" observed at GugaS'thebe is a socially embedded, community-based process driven from below rather than from the top. This is what makes the space work. Mentors and programme managers are locals from the community · and this has proved to be important for the sustainability of the space. The space is managed by the City of Cape Town.

At the time that this research was undertaken, facilitators appointed by the City have proved to be responsive to the needs of the community and fulfilled the role of creative intermediaries well. However, staff turnover at the City and changes in funding do pose risks for the future viability of GugaS'thebe. Broader social impacts flowing from the activities at GugaS'thebe are outlined subsequently.

GugaS'thebe Crafters Association

The GugaS'thebe Crafters Association was formed in 2011 by the tenants occupying the cultural centre who had a desire to be included in operational and strategic matters of the centre. A group of older women (beading and weaving crafters) participated in our focus group and spoke as representatives of the GugaS'thebe Crafters Association, of which they are members. The women saw themselves as social entrepreneurs who are passionate about ploughing back into their community. While the primary purpose of the group is to present a voice for the tenants of GugaS'thebe, they are also active in building the social fabric in Langa, promoting education and skills training and encouraging social responsibility as important aspects of their role in the community. Their activities are outlined below in more detail:

- Representing the GugaS'thebe tenants and community by listening, understanding and acting according to the needs of its members
- Providing leadership and enabling GugaS'thebe crafters to speak with a unified voice on matters that affect them
- Offering skills training in beading and sewing to children from a local school. This initiative was however discontinued for the time being because of a lack of funds, but the women are keen to take this up again
- Initiating events to promote social cohesion and intergenerational discourse towards tackling social ills in their community. One event is that of the "War Rooms" – a group of boys meet in a room with older men, while a group of girls meet in a room with older women for an hour. The youths raise any issues and concerns that they may have and discuss these with the elders; the issues are discussed without interruption and without anyone leaving the room. The issues discussed remain in the room and the communication is horizontal. Elders relinquish their "authority" and commit to engage at the level of each participant, without intimidation. A person is placed outside the door at each venue, keeping watch for potential disturbances. After the session ends, youths and elders are brought into a larger venue where they are met by government officials, including facilitators, social workers, police officers, etc. The officials are asked to prepare presentations on specific topic and to facilitate an interactive session for the youths and the elders on issues ranging from crime prevention to reproductive health education. Another event, centred on food and entertainment, occurs in Women's Month (August) for female children and elders
- Assisting the elderly, a group most vulnerable to violence and depression in black communities. One programme involves training children in drama, dance and music. Pensioners from the community are then invited to be entertained by the learners and treated to a meal prepared by the GugaS'thebe family. This interesting programme brings together two generations separated by age and life experiences to allow for an exchange of ideas and perspectives as the elderly interact with the youths during the session.

Our Workshop

Our Workshop is an initiative started by acclaimed South African designer Heath Nash with the intention of creating a shared workshop space in which aspiring designers and emerging crafters can explore their creativity and engage in design-led thinking processes to overcome their situational challenges. An informal programme runs through the workshop space, creating a platform for local designers to explore, to share their skills and also to be empowered through working collaboratively. The shared workshop space has recently become a magnet for young creatives and unemployed youths to "hang out" to inadvertently be drawn into entrepreneurship and design processes. Examples of creative work include wire craft and the making of furniture using recycled or upcycled materials.

Performing arts programmes

Dance by Jika Madinga

Local dance star Thabisa Dinga offers free dance classes to young aspiring dancers in GugaS'thebe's dance room, located above the workshops, on a weekly basis. The self-funded programme aims to develop these young girls emotionally and physically through classes strongly supported by an integrated mentorship programme to boost self-esteem and to foster an understanding of teamwork and individual responsibility.

Capoeira

In the light of frequent xenophobic attacks on foreign nationals in township areas in 2016, a group of Angolan immigrants living in Langa approached GugaS'thebe with a cultural exchange programme in an attempt to build social cohesion. Angolan instructors facilitate weekly capoeira dance with up to 100 local participants. The dance studio space is also used for yoga sessions.

Drumming

One of the most popular programmes in the centre is a schools-based programme for learners from schools in the Langa community. The programme offers drumming lessons to learners at no cost. Learners are exposed to West African drumming techniques after school, curbing youth idleness and vulnerability to substance abuse and gang culture. This programme is supported by crafters and artists through donations which go towards providing snack packs to the learners.

Outdoor theatre

GugaS'thebe also has performance art spaces (Figure 9.4) utilised by local dance groups. School groups are exposed to the diverse world

Figure 9.4 Performance art space at GugaS'thebe.

of performing through also being featured at local and international festivals, allowing them to gain experience and build their own portfolios in the industry.

GugaS'thebe as a tourism space

GugaS'thebe is frequented by tourists, predominantly foreign visitors. Crafters at GugaS'thebe mostly sell to tourists at the centre or elsewhere in Cape Town, i.e. pop-up markets at the V&A Waterfront. However, for most crafts the tourism market ensures seasonal business. Certain young entrepreneurs are able to offer Airbnb experiences to diversify their incomes. The visitor market mostly consists of young tourists who are interested in arts, craft and heritage experiences, while older tourists reportedly undertake traditional township tours. Examples of creative experiences include street-art walking tours, visiting the Langa Pass Office Museum with a local who provides historical context, making a pair of earrings instead of simply buying them, participating in drumming sessions, etc. These experiences are said to be profitable for the crafters and artists at GugaS'thebe, and they allow cultural practitioners to connect with the global community through participatory culture-based experiences.

Conclusion

Langa as a place functions as a curative hub for the long and rich histories of Eastern Xhosa migration to the city of Cape Town. Its history is part and parcel of the heritage and culture of the township and its rich historical narrative is the focal point of many of tourism offerings. Within this environment, GugaS'thebe is a compelling example of a creative space which not only serves as a makerspace for local creatives, but also stimulates a number of social and developmental spinoffs. This is ascribed to social embeddedness and entrepreneurship supported by community-based organisations, NPOs and the City of Cape Town as intermediaries. Indeed, Brown (2017: 13) avers with reference to coworking spaces that: "More equitably distributed benefits and positive social impacts have been observed with bottom-up, grass-roots approaches, typically where non-profit and small-scale local arts mix with small-scale commercial cultural and creative enterprises". The success and sustainability of GugaS'thebe, furthermore, rest on the sustained grassroots involvement of locals, which contributes to a sense of community ownership of the space. This differs from top-down creative planning interventions which more often than not fail in the long run (see Brown 2017). The role of creative workers is also illuminating; they are not only crafters/designers or artists; but also mentors, facilitators of skills training and community workers. Moreover, facilitators appointed by the City have fulfilled their roles as creative intermediaries well.

GugaS'thebe is not a typical incubator through which young entrepreneurs come up and move out. There is a critical mass of local creative workers who are permanently involved and who keep it all together. Notwithstanding, the space should support different life and career pathways or trajectories for individuals and it should be recognised that the individuals' measures of success differ. In other words, young entrepreneurs who want to expand and move on should be supported. However, support for entrepreneurs who leave incubator programmes is often not forthcoming in South Africa. Permanent creative workers, mostly older women, have a wider social development vision and have support from community-based organisations with a wider mandate. GugaS'thebe is a platform for some of their activities. It should however be mentioned that some community-based organisations are more active than others and some lack staying power.

The emphasis at GugaS'thebe is art, culture and heritage and not necessarily digital technologies, as is often the case in coworking spaces (Brown, 2017; Smith, 2017). The centre can also be regarded as a makerspace (see Smith, 2017), although a focus on digital design and production is not the priority. GugaS'thebe is an intergenerational space compared to coworking spaces typically occupied by young entrepreneurs and independent creative professionals (Brown, 2017). Workers at the centre are self-organising, and social capital, local embeddedness and networks and a sense of community are integral to the success of the space not only commercially, but also for achieving social development outcomes. This corresponds with the experience of other coworking spaces and creative city dynamics (Brown, 2017; Comunian, 2011; Gandini, 2015; Smith, 2017).

The emphasis on art (murals and mosaics) to curate a place narrative corresponds with Marques and Richards (2014). This is significant for placemaking which goes beyond creative city marketing or branding. Street art in Langa is socially embedded, curating its rich cultural and heritage stories. This is important for locals in terms of belonging, remembrance and heritage preservation. However, street art also has visitor appeal and education value.

It is recognised that not all stakeholders are necessarily in favour of the development of GugaS'thebe as a tourism space as intended by the City. This said, certain locals benefit from tourism and are positive about it and the area is largely welcoming to visitors. We suggest that tourism consumption emerged because of the demand for township tourism by foreign visitors. We also propose that centres like GugaS'thebe can be developed as a multi-purpose centre and that it holds potential for stimulating broader creative and tourism precinct development. It is argued that a greater focus on tourism can afford direct benefits to locals and open up opportunities for other tourism services like restaurants, shops, attractions and experiences which diversify the tourism mix. The heritage resources in Langa like the Pass Office Museum and Old Post Office are underdeveloped as tourism attractions and are also underutilised as heritage spaces. Creative tourism and creative placemaking should also stimulate physical upgrading in Langa (Booyens and Rogerson, 2019a). In addition, creative forms of tourism in townships are alternatives to more voyeuristic forms of poverty tourism (see Booyens and Rogerson, 2019a, 2019b; George and Booyens, 2014).

Acknowledgements

This work forms part of the activities of the research network *Understanding and Supporting Creative Economies in Africa: Education, Networks and Policy* spearheaded by Dr Roberta Comunian, King's College London and Dr Brian J. Hracs, University of Southampton.

This research network is supported by the Arts and Humanities Research Council (United Kingdom). We thank the reviewers for their helpful comments on an earlier version of this text.

References

Adamo G.E., Ferrari S. and Gilli M. (2019) Creativity as a source of differentiation in urban tourism: the case of Torino city. *International Journal of Tourism Research* 21(3): 302–310.

Beavon K. and Rogerson C.M. (1990) Temporary trading for temporary people: the making of hawking in Soweto. In: Drakakis-Smith D. (ed.) *Economic Growth and Urbanization in Developing Areas.* London: Routledge, pp. 263–286.

Booyens I. (2010) Rethinking township tourism: towards responsible tourism development in South African townships. *Development Southern Africa* 27: 273–287.

Booyens I. and Rogerson C.M. (2015) Creative tourism in Cape Town: an innovation perspective. *Urban Forum* 6(4): 405–424.

Booyens I. and Rogerson C.M. (2019a) Creative tourism: South African township explorations. *Tourism Review* 74(2): 256–267.

Booyens I. and Rogerson C.M. (2019b) Recreating slum tourism: perspectives from South Africa. *Urbani izziv* 30: S52–S63.

Brown J. (2017). Curating the "third place"? Coworking and the mediation of creativity. *Geoforum* 82: 112–126.

Choplin A. (2016) Rethinking precarious neighbourhoods, rethinking the future city. In: Deboulet A. (ed.) *Rethinking Precarious Neighbourhoods.* Paris: Agence Française de Développement, pp. 245–250.

City of Cape Town (2016) Re-imaging GugaS'thebe and Langa Museum (Langa Cultural Precinct/District). Cape Town: City of Cape Town, Arts and Culture Department.

Coetzer N. (2009) *Langa Township in the 1920s – An (Extra) Ordinary Garden Suburb.* PhD thesis, University of Cape Town, South Africa.

Comunian R. (2011) Rethinking the creative city: the role of complexity, networks and interactions in the urban creative economy. *Urban Studies* 48(6): 1157–1179.

Dovey K. and King R. (2012) Informal urbanism and the taste for slums. *Tourism Geographies* 14(2): 275–293.

Drummond F. and Snowball J. (2019) Cultural clusters as a local economic development strategy in rural small-town areas: Sarah Baartman District in South Africa. *Bulletin of Geography. Socio-economic Series* 43(43): 107–119.

Duxbury N., Hosagrahar J. and Pascual J. (2016) *Why Must Culture be at the Heart of Sustainable Urban Development? Agenda 21 for Culture.* Buenos Aires: Committee on Culture of United Cities and Local Governments.

Frenzel F. (2016) *Slumming It: The Tourist Valorization of Urban Poverty.* London: Zed.

Gandini A. (2015) The rise of coworking spaces: a literature review. *ephemera* 15(1): 193–205.

George R. and Booyens I. (2014) Township tourism demand: tourists' perceptions of safety and security. *Urban Forum* 25(4): 449–467.

Giliomee H.B. and Mbenga B. (2007) *New History of South Africa*. Cape Town: Tafelberg.

Gregory J.J. and Rogerson C.M. (2018) Suburban creativity: the geography of creative industries in Johannesburg. *Bulletin of Geography. Socio-economic Series* 39(39): 31–52.

Jürgens U. and Donaldson R. (2012) A review of literature on transformation processes in South African townships. *Urban Forum* 23(2): 153–163.

Marques L. and Richards G. (2014) The dimensions of art in place narrative. *Tourism Planning and Development* 11(1): 1–12.

Minty Z. and Nkula-Wenz L (2019) Effecting cultural change from below? A comparison of Cape Town and Bandung's pathways to urban cultural governance. *Cultural Trends* 28(4): 281–293.

Moriset. B (2014) Building new places of the creative economy. The rise of coworking spaces. HAL Id: halshs-00914075. Presented at the 2nd Geography of Innovation International Conference 2014, Utrecht University, Utrecht, The Netherlands, January 23–25 2014.

Oyekunle O.A. (2017) The contribution of creative industries to sustainable urban development in South Africa. *African Journal of Science, Technology, Innovation and Development* 9(5): 607–616.

Pieterse E. (2011) Grasping the unknowable: coming to grips with African urbanisms. *Social Dynamics* 37(1): 5–23.

Richards G. (2018) Tourism, an underestimated driving force for the creative economy. *Revista Turismo em Análise* 29(3): 387–395.

Smith A. (2017) Social Innovation, Democracy and Makerspaces. Science Policy Research Unit (SPRU) Working Paper SWPS 2017–10. Brighton: University of Sussex.

United Nations Conference on Trade and Development (2011) Strengthening the Creative Industries for Development in Mozambique. New York: United Nations.

10 Conclusions

Lauren England, Brian J. Hracs and Roberta Comunian

This book has brought together a range of perspectives and reflections on the spaces and working practices that inform the development of creative economies in Africa. We would like to conclude the book by teasing out some broader themes and presenting recommendations for the development of creative economies in Africa based on the contributions and our research project. Our considerations focus on four areas: the importance of networks, funding and engaged policy frameworks in supporting creative economies; coworking spaces as platforms for entrepreneurship but also empowerment; how clusters and creative spaces connect across cultural, economic and social development agendas; and finally, the role of women and platforms to support women in the development of Africa's creative economies. Building on the collective recommendations of the authors, we provide three policy reflections which we hope will be useful to creative economy leaders and policymakers working in this field.

Developing creative economies through networks, funding and mutual learning

The first three chapters of the book highlight the varied working practices and experiences of creatives which in part reflect the diversity of the creative and cultural industries (CCIs) but also the specificities of the national and local contexts in which they operate. A number of common challenges are nevertheless identifiable, including isolated working practices and a lack of mentorship and collaboration opportunities, limited access to formal and consistent funding, networks to support the exchange of ideas, knowledge and resources, social support for pursuing a creative career and policy support. Building on reflections on the role of policy developed in our first edited book (Comunian et al., 2021), there is also a general sense that the CCIs

DOI: 10.4324/9781003191681-10

have not been prioritised, or have even been neglected by policymakers, with critique levied against initiatives seen to pay lip service to creative economy development (Chapter 2) and a lack of investment in creative education and engagement with artists (Chapter 3). Nevertheless, the authors also emphasise how creatives have built thriving careers, often by taking matters into their own hands, presenting valuable opportunities for governments to learn from their entrepreneurial instincts in developing policies for creative economy development. This includes the adoption of diversification strategies (Chapter 2), tapping into a range of national, transnational and international funding and working across a number of formal and informal markets (Chapter 3). While the need for further financing and market development assistance is echoed across these chapters, it is nevertheless acknowledged that the entrepreneurial activities of creatives has facilitated the development of a vibrant industry. Such atypical development models present valuable learning opportunities, both as proof of concept for domestic initiatives to support cultural development and for Global North countries in how to create new sources of revenue, employment and growth that can support profitable and sustainable CCIs (Lobato, 2010).

The development of HEVA articulated in Chapter 4 also highlights innovation in CCI funding models which support growth and value-adding business optimisation and production efficiencies. The framework for this creative intermediary (Comunian et al., 2022) is currently being expanded beyond Kenya and presents a model for CCI development with relevance across the continent and beyond. However, while the CCIs are commonly valued for their potential for job creation and contribution to gross domestic product (GDP), and a number of the observations and recommendations presented in this book speak to this, it is also important to note that these are not always the values pursued by creatives (Chapters 2 and 3). Their entrepreneurial endeavours may prioritise sustainability over scaling up and artistic and cultural expression over income generation.

Creatives also have a role to play in educating the government about what support they need (Chapters 2 and 3) and in demonstrating best practice and innovative approaches to finance (Chapter 4) from within the sector. Best practice can develop in a relatively short period of time, through both international collaborations and the work of local intermediaries (Comunian et al., 2022). Building on the research developed in book 1 on the role of both top-down cultural policy and bottom-up initiatives for creative economies in Africa (Comunian et al., 2021), the chapters here stress the necessity of bringing creatives and policymakers together (Chapters 2 and 3) and how enhanced data on CCIs in Africa can support evidence-based policy making (Chapter 4). Combined, these chapters make a valuable contribution to our understanding of how creatives make a living. This helps to address the lack of data on CCIs in Africa, which has so far been a major challenge for government and other stakeholders in creating targeted programmes and policies for CCIs. Examples of best practice presented in these chapters from East and West Africa may also facilitate wider learning across the continent.

Coworking as a tool for economic development and empowerment

The second theme emerging is the role of coworking spaces in Africa as a tool for both economic development and social empowerment. The reflections in Chapters 5 to 7 add valuable African perspectives to the limited literature and research on coworking in the Global South (Tintiangko and Soriano, 2020). The rise in coworking, incubation and business development support corresponds with a growing demand for informal learning settings and activities that enhance collaboration, social networking and community development. However, they can also facilitate societal changes with broader impact (Akanle and Omotayo, 2020). This includes economic empowerment, but also supporting particular groups in society who may otherwise be excluded from business development opportunities such as women, as discussed by England et al. (Chapter 6). These chapters therefore help to extend our understanding of the continuum of "third spaces" in which coworking sits (Brown, 2017), and highlight their connection with both economic and social development agendas. However, there currently appears to be a lack of strategic correlation between cultural and urban policies in relation to coworking and creative hubs (Chapter 7). Again, a number of challenges in securing the sustainability of coworking spaces in Africa are highlighted, including financing and the prominence of private-sector initiatives, which has implications for consistency in growth and accessibility.

It is also important that the development of spaces to support economic development empower society at large rather than preserving benefits for the few. As reflected on by Wangusa et al. in Chapter 7, Covid-19 may disrupt collective working models and undermine exchanges and collaboration across CCIs and creative workers. They nevertheless argue that, even with this challenging context ahead, creative hubs could offer vital support to creatives whose working practices have been dramatically affected by the pandemic (Comunian and England, 2020) and provide a collaborative environment for African cities to re-think their post-Covid-19 future and for urban and national policy to further coordinate their agenda with the creative economy.

Connecting across culture, economic and social development

Creativity is central to contemporary urban development and placemaking approaches (Minty and Nkula-Wenz, 2019) (Figure 10.1), and culture has often been employed as a resource for creative endeavours to support job creation and poverty reduction, skills training and social upliftment (Duxbury et al., 2016). The reflections of the third section of this book (Chapters 8 and 9) reveal the coming together of cultural, social and economic development agendas within Africa's creative spaces and clusters. The chapters highlight the varied activities that are conducted in coworking and other creative spaces in Africa, including cultural production and work that emphasises heritage and community development, and which also supports tourism. Creative spaces and

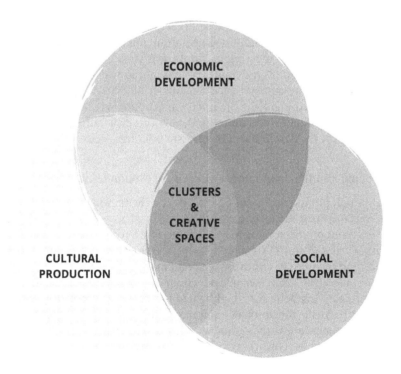

Figure 10.1 Clusters and creative spaces at the intersection of cultural, economic and social development.

clusters also cater to diverse communities and localities, including small rural towns (Chapter 8) and townships (Chapter 9).

This collection highlights the range of creative spaces which help to form and sustain Africa's creative ecology. The multifunctionality of coworking spaces discussed above is further developed in creative clusters and spaces. Booyens et al.'s (Chapter 9) case of GugaS'thebe Cultural Centre highlights how the centre not only serves as a makerspace for local creatives, but also stimulates developmental spinoffs, including creative tourism, and promotes social cohesion and intergenerational discourse aimed at tackling social ills in their community. Here social embeddedness and entrepreneurship are supported by a range of individuals and intermediaries (Comunian et al., 2022) but are driven and sustained by a grassroots community and a critical mass of local creative workers. It is also important to note that creative economy development initiatives are place-specific, and not limited to urban areas. Rural areas (Chapter 8) and townships (Chapter 9), which may lack the breadth of infrastructure and human capital to develop a diverse range of CCIs, also have specific dynamics which must be taken into account. Drummond and Snowball (Chapter 8) note that not all types of CCIs are suited to small-town operation, nor are they suited to every small town. Rather, they argue, rural town strategies should build on existing CCIs clusters and focus on activities in which there is already a comparative advantage (Fleischmann et al., 2017). Booyens et al. (Chapter 9) also highlight the interconnection of creative spaces with their local heritage and culture and how this rich historical narrative can support the development of tourism offerings.

Women and the development of creative economies in Africa

Although not a direct focus of the book, a theme which emerged from across the three sections relates to the work of women in Africa's creative economy. Sectors of the CCIs with low barriers to entry (such as visual arts and crafts) are already recognised for their potential to create jobs and income for disadvantaged and marginalised people (Abisuga-Oyekunle et al., 2021), many of whom are women (Chapter 8). The chapters in this book have highlighted further areas – potentially with higher barriers (educational, equipment and capital requirements) – in which women are thriving and driving development – as filmmakers (Chapter 2), in coworking spaces (Chapter 6) and through creative community work (Chapter 9). This is despite entrepreneurial barriers (Anambane and Adom, 2018) and marginalisation politically

(Chapter 6) and socially in accessing business support (Chapters 3 and 6) or within global industries (Chapter 2). They also spotlight a number of formal and informal initiatives targeted towards women, such as funding frameworks (Chapter 4) and coworking spaces (Chapter 6). Here creative spaces and local community structures provide a platform for both entrepreneurial and socially orientated activities (Chapter 9). Collectively, these chapters present a number of different platforms which enable women entrepreneurs to access capacity building, business support and mentorship opportunities in more formalised economies. These contributions highlight the importance of studying industries and contexts (formal and informal) where women have been successful and the platforms which support them. In developing creative economies and expanding international engagement with African CCIs, it is imperative that the conditions which support women entrepreneurs are fostered and that – as cautioned by Steedman in Chapter 2 – growth and internationalisation do not make it harder for women to climb the ladder.

Policy reflections for cultural leaders and policymakers

The chapters in this book not only present broader analyses of trends in East, West and South Africa (coworking and creative hubs) but also provide valuable insights from national contexts (specifically Nigeria, Kenya and South Africa) and place-specific analysis in both urban and rural contexts. In addressing these three spatial levels, the contributions of this book highlight broader trends which can be used to inform continental agendas and policymaking, as well as develop richer understandings of CCIs activity which can support realistic and effective regional cultural policymaking that builds on existing comparative advantage and is place-specific. The chapters have also highlighted how CCIs, the creatives within them and their infrastructure, have so far developed largely outside of policy support. Equally, they all call for this relationship to be re-evaluated and for creative economies to be recognised and their activities to be anchored within urban policies and city master plans to enhance sustainable development. Building on their collective recommendations, these reflections are presented as possible policy directions for creative economy leaders and policymakers to support the development of sustainable creative economies in Africa. While some might be more or less applicable in each context or locality and should be tailored to place specifics, we hope they remain broadly relevant.

Bringing together policymakers and entrepreneurs to develop effective, experience-based strategies for creative economies

There are significant opportunities for governments to learn from their creative communities and their entrepreneurial strategies. The voices of creatives need to be heard in developing policies for the creative economy in order to create strategies and support systems that directly respond to the needs of the sector. By developing forums for creatives and intermediary organisations to actively contribute to policymaking, policymakers will benefit from the deep knowledge within the CCIs of the models that *already* work. This can be further supported by facilitating more research into CCIs to support evidence-based decision making. A connected agenda for cultural, economic and social development is also key to capitalise on the intersections between these areas and to draw on the combined efforts of creative entrepreneurs, private, public and third-sector intermediaries (see the final recommendation, below) and their wider links beyond the creative economy.

Creating accessible and inclusive infrastructure to support creative economies

National and continental-level support is needed to create accessible and inclusive infrastructure for the creative economy. This would address the existing challenges in developing creative spaces and supporting the working lives of creatives across Africa, including financial constraints, educational provision (Comunian et al., 2021), poor infrastructure and low levels of access to technology. It would also facilitate the internationalisation and market development of Africa's diverse creative products through international distribution and domestic tourism opportunities. By expanding the educational base for creatives – creatively and entrepreneurially – there is the opportunity not only to support domestic activities but to facilitate gains in the international recognition, appreciation and valuation of African CCIs outputs. It is also important that policymakers and creative economy stakeholders recognise, support and continue to grow the diversity of creatives, CCIs business models and spaces that support them, including those that address the specific needs of marginalised or underrepresented groups.

Developing partnership models and multi-stakeholder collaborations to support sustainable creative economies

Partnerships and multi-stakeholder collaborations across private, third-sector/community and public organisations can address the limited longevity of top-down initiatives (Brown, 2017) and may provide the most sustainable model for creative economy and infrastructure development. This includes developing the local embeddedness and critical mass of actors needed to initiate, develop and sustain creative careers, clusters and spaces in the long term. Initiatives should support both the economic and wider cultural and social development aspects of creative work, and the spaces in which it takes place, in order to create a vibrant ecosystem that thrives and can also provide opportunities for the wider population and be accessible across socio-economic classes.

References

Abisuga-Oyekunle O.A., England L. and Comunian R. (2021) Developing the handicraft sector in South Africa. In: Comunian R., Hracs B.J. and England L. (eds) *Higher Education and Policy for Creative Economies in Africa: Developing Creative Economies*. London: Routledge, pp. 131–150.

Akanle O. and Omotayo A. (2020) Youth, unemployment and incubation hubs in Southwest Nigeria. *African Journal of Science, Technology, Innovation and Development* 12: 165–172.

Anambane G. and Adom K. (2018) Assessing the role of culture in female entrepreneurship in contemporary sub-Saharan society: insights from the Nabadam district of Ghana. *Journal of Developmental Entrepreneurship* 23: 1850017.

Brown J. (2017) Curating the "third place"? Coworking and the mediation of creativity. *Geoforum* 82: 112–126.

Comunian R. and England L. (2020) Creative and cultural work without filters: Covid-19 and exposed precarity in the creative economy. *Cultural Trends* 29: 112–128.

Comunian R., Hracs B.J. and England L. (2021) *Higher Education and Policy for Creative Economies in Africa: Developing Creative Economies*. London: Routledge.

Comunian R., Hracs B.J. and England L. (2022) Cultural intermediaries revisited: lessons from Cape Town, Lagos and Nairobi. In: Hracs B.J., Brydges T., Haisch T., et al. (eds) *Culture, Creativity and Economy: Collaborative Practices, Value Creation and Spaces of Creativity*. London: Routledge.

Duxbury N., Hosagrahar J. and Pascual J. (2016) Why must culture be at the heart of sustainable urban development? *Agenda 21 for Culture*. Barcelona: Committee on Culture of United Cities and Local Governments (UCLG).

Fleischmann K., Daniel R. and Welters R. (2017) Developing a regional economy through creative industries: innovation capacity in a regional Australian city. *Creative Industries Journal* 10: 119–138.

Lobato R. (2010) Creative industries and informal economies: lessons from Nollywood. *International Journal of Cultural Studies* 13: 337–354.

Minty Z. and Nkula-Wenz L. (2019) Effecting cultural change from below? A comparison of Cape Town and Bandung's pathways to urban cultural governance. *Cultural Trends* 28: 281–293.

Nakano D., Shiach M., Koria M., et al. (2020) Coworking spaces in urban settings: prospective roles? *Geoforum* 115: 135–137.

Tintiangko J. and Soriano C.R. (2020) Coworking spaces in the global south: local articulations and imaginaries. *Journal of Urban Technology* 27: 67–85.

Index

Printed in the United States
by Baker & Taylor Publisher Services